W9-BNH-432

{ speaking in styles }

FUNDAMENTALS OF CSS *for* WEB DESIGNERS

jason cranford teague

New Riders

VOICES THAT MATTER™

Speaking in Styles

Fundamentals of CSS for Web Designers

Jason Cranford Teague

Project Editor:
Nancy Peterson

Development Editor:
Brenda McLaughlin

Technical Editor:
Dave Artz

**Production
Coordinator:**
Cory Borman

Copy Editors:
Dan Foster,
Darren Meiss

Compositor:
Jason Cranford Teague

Marketing Manager:
Glenn Bisignani

Indexer: Emily
Glossbrenner

**Cover and Interior
Designer:**
Jason Cranford Teague

Cover Production:
Andreas DeDanaan

New Riders

1249 Eighth Street

Berkeley, CA 94710

510/524-2178

Find us on the Web at www.newriders.com

To report errors, please send a note to errata@peachpit.com

New Riders is an imprint of Peachpit, a division of Pearson Education

Copyright © 2009 Jason Cranford Teague

Notice of Rights

All rights reserved. No part of this book may be reproduced or transmitted in any form by any means, electronic, mechanical, photocopying, recording, or otherwise, without the prior written permission of the publisher. For information on getting permission for reprints and excerpts, contact permissions@peachpit.com.

Notice of Liability

The information in this book is distributed on an "As Is" basis without warranty. While every precaution has been taken in the preparation of the book, neither the author nor Peachpit shall have any liability to any person or entity with respect to any loss or damage caused or alleged to be caused directly or indirectly by the instructions contained in this book or by the computer software and hardware products described in it.

Trademarks

Many of the designations used by manufacturers and sellers to distinguish their products are claimed as trademarks. Where those designations appear in this book, and Peachpit was aware of a trademark claim, the designations appear as requested by the owner of the trademark. All other product names and services identified throughout this book are used in editorial fashion only and for the benefit of such companies with no intention of infringement of the trademark. No such use, or the use of any trade name, is intended to convey endorsement or other affiliation with this book.

Printed and bound in the United States of America

ISBN 13: 978-0-321-57416-9

ISBN 10: 0-321-57416-8

9 8 7 6 5 4 3 2 1

Printed and bound in the United States of America

In Memory of

Mossie Stone Teague

&

Oscar Brantley Teague

Thanks...

Tara

Dashiel & Jocelyn

Dad & Nancy

Johnny

Pat & Red

Boyd, Dr. G, & Judy

Thomas, Archer, & David

Charles Dodgson & John Tenniel

Douglas Adams & Carl Sagan

Neil Gaimen & Dave McKean

The noise that kept me going...

NPR, Ted Talks, Skepticality, Slice of Sci-fi,
The Craig Charles Funk & Soul Show, Bat for
Lashes, Amanda Palmer (AFP), Wilson Pickett,
Carbon/Silicon, Scissor Sisters, Kate Bush,
Bryan Ferry, The Fixx, Jonathan Coulton,
Cranes, Johnny Cash, Cocteau Twins, Ladytron,
Marvin Gaye, Client, Cracker, Corduroy, Al
Green, The Wombats, Electric Six, World Party,
Skinny Puppy, The Cramps, Poprocket, Franz
Ferdinand, The Long Blondes, Gogol Bordello,
Mojo Nixon, Beck, and The Specials.

Contents

PART 2 CSS Grammer

PART 3 Speaking Like a Native

APPENDIXES

INTRODUCTION

To design is to communicate clearly by whatever means you can control or master.

— *Milton Glaser*

Design is a way to communicate ideas visually. Unlike speaking or writing, however, visual communication happens almost instantaneously on a visceral level. Within seconds of seeing something, we should be able to understand its visual message. Obviously some designs such as illustrations may take additional deciphering, but when we look at something we can't help trying to interpret its meaning.

Although Web design is a visual medium, it is created using written code—a style language known as CSS. While you can use programs like Adobe Photoshop or Dreamweaver to take a design and output the code, this rarely produces desirable results. To get the best results for your designs, you need to learn how to speak in styles.

INTRODUCTION

Verbalizing the Visual

I want you to think of a shape. It can be any shape you want—a circle, a square, a triangle, an eight-pointed star, or an ameboid glob—but keep it to a single continuous shape. I want you to hold that shape in your mind, or, if you need to, scratch it out on a piece of paper (or, if you are really far gone) on a computer.

Now I want you to think about how you would describe the shape without making reference to any shape. You can use "line," but not any shape names.

Let's say you draw a simple square. You might describe a square like this:

Draw four lines the same length that touch, two horizontally and two vertically.

This sounds accurate. If I were drawing the shape as you described it, I might draw a square:

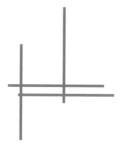

However, following the same directions, I might draw something completely different:

I've been teaching CSS for several years now, and every time I perform this exercise with students, they are amused (and frustrated) when I follow their directions but end up with a shape that looks nothing like what they are trying to describe. The problem isn't with them, however; the problem is that humans make a lot of assumptions when it comes to communication. We are not just following the stated directions; we are also calculating what the person giving the directions is actually thinking. We fill in missing details, such as that all four lines should touch *at their ends*.

As good as they are becoming at understanding humans, computers still require that we communicate explicitly when we describe something, especially when that something is a visual design. A computer will not fill in the details.

What is needed is a language that you can use to quickly and precisely describe your designs in such a way that the computer will understand them without fault. That language is called Cascading Style Sheets (CSS), and it is a language you need to master to be a successful Web designer.

Why CSS?

Cascading Style Sheets (CSS) is the language you use to tell computers how you want your designs to look on the Web. With CSS, you can specify details including widths, heights, colors, margins, padding, borders, backgrounds, and type styles. Understanding this language, then, becomes critical to achieving the best online designs.

One of the constant complaints I hear from designers is that developers never execute their design correctly. Learning CSS gives you two important advantages as a designer:

01 **Control over how your designs look online**. If something is the wrong color or is not lining up right, you will know what is wrong and how to fix it.

02 **The ability to create better Web designs**. Knowing how CSS works means knowing how to get the best results from what is possible.

The good news is that speaking CSS is not that different from speaking in English or any other "human" language—it just takes a little adjustment to get used to its particular syntax (how things are said), semantics (what things mean), and vocabulary (what to say).

For example, consider this simple design:

To describe this design in English, you might say something like:

The border is solid red and 5 pixels thick; the background is pink; there is a 25 pixel padding around the content; the font is Arial at 8 pixels; and the text is double spaced.

The same description in CSS isn't actually that different:

border: 5px solid red;
background-color: pink;
padding: 25px;
font: 8px/2 arial;

Notice that most of the words (vocabulary) are almost identical. It's primarily the structure (syntax) that's different, but it's really not that hard to decipher.

The goal of this book is to teach you to be able to describe your Web designs as easily in CSS as you do in English.

Reading This Book

I wrote this book for designers of all stripes—visual, interactive, user experience, information architecture. However, it is really for anyone who wants to learn how to use CSS.

Speaking in Styles is split into three sections and includes three appendixes:

- **Part 1: A Web Primer**
  Defines what makes a Web page, introduces some tools you will need to build one, and dispels some popular myths about designers and CSS.

- **Part 2: CSS Grammar**
  Covers the nuts and bolts of how to create style sheets and apply them to a Web page, including the important vocabulary designers need to know.

- **Part 3: Speaking Like a Native**
  Follows the creation of a simple Web page design, emphasizing the best practices you should use.

- **Appendixes**
  Includes all of the code for Part 3; the length, font, and color values you use with CSS; and a list of common fixes for dealing with the bugs in Internet Explorer.

Reading the Code

I have tried to simplify the examples as much as possible, keeping code and the results of that code as close as possible on the page. This often means that the full context of the code is not given.

The code is colored based on use:

Content in code
HTML code
CSS code
JavaScript code

Where I have included longer blocks of code, I have numbered the individual lines:

```
01  <style type="text/css" media="all">
02  h1 { color: red; }
03  </style>
```

Code references in the text will look like (01-03), and the referenced code will always be on the same page or on the page immediately to the right.

Browser Abbreviations and Versions

NAME	ABBREVIATION	ACTIVE VERSIONS
Internet Explorer	IE	6, 7, 8
Firefox	FF	3, 4
Safari	Sa	3, 4
Opera	Op	8, 9, 10
Chrome	Ch	1, 2

PART 1

In which the reader will learn about the three core components of a Web page, discover the tools needed to construct one, and uncover the truth about many Web page myths.

A Web Primer

{ speaking in styles }

A CSS PRIMER *for* WEB DESIGNERS

Welcome

Cover Concept

Speaking In Styles is the forthcoming book by Jason Cranford Teague to help designers better understand how they can use CSS to create their designs for the Web.

More About *Speaking In Styles* →

Jason Interviewed on Peachpit TV

Posted on *February 19th, 2009* by jason

Read more →

Pontificating about the future.

Tags: Conferences, Future, Internet // Add Comment »

Transparent PNGs (Yes, Even in IE6)

Posted on *September 19th, 2008* by jason

It will be a glorious day in the world of the Web when Internet Explorer 6 is completely abolished from every computer everywhere. I will not read from the litany of charges against this most sinister of Web applications; my own chief gripe has to do with how Microsoft implemented the PNG-24 format, and how their slip-shod work has held back the visual possibilities in Web design (without using Flash) for over 5 years.

Read more →

Tags: Web Graphics // 1 Comment »

Jason Interviewed by WOW

Posted on *July 11th, 2008* by jason

At the recent Voices that Matter conference, I had the privilege of having dinner with Bill Cullifer, the Executive Director of WOW (World Organization of Webmasters). I hadn't check in with that group in a while (they've been around since 1996), so I was excited to

WHERE I'M SPEAKING...

SxSW Interactive
Austin, Tx | Online Comics & a reading from *Speaking In Styles*.
17 Mar 2009 03:30 PM | more ›

Voices That Matter
San Francisco, Ca | Web Typography and Designing Credibility. Use the code **WBASPKR** to get a $200 discount.
27 Apr 2009 | more ›

WHAT I'M DOING...

Just In: I'm going to be reading from my forth coming book _Speaking In Styles_ @SXSW (#SX09-4648) http://tinyurl.com/blvfb3 5 hrs ago

Whovians rejoice! Acclaimed Doctor Who author Simon Guerrier is now twittering under the handle @Otralala. In reply to Otralala 9 hrs ago

thinks @taracranford "nice voice" sounds very, very (very) sarcastic. 23 hrs ago

More updates...

WEBBEDENVIRONMENT

I'm On (peachpit) TV!

WATCHMEN: Now With Motion!

Heavy Liquid: Cyberpunk in the cyber age.

The Spirit is Just a Plain Fun Movie

Catching Up With JCT: Yuri's Night

SXSW

Don't Forget the ScreenBurn at SXSW Arcade = Free (as in Money and Information)

PAGES

Contact
Inspirations
The Author
The Book

RECENT POSTS

Jason Interviewed on Peachpit TV
Transparent PNGs (Yes, Even in IE6)
Jason Interviewed by WOW
Browser Safe Fonts: Beta Available!
See You at Voices That Matter

CATEGORIES

Conferences (3)
Future (1)
Internet (1)
Typography (4)
Web Graphics (1)

CULTURE SITES

webbedENVIRONMENTS

DESIGN SITES

WordPress Planet

Take a look behind a Web page, any Web page, and you'll find that it's a combination of just three types of code: HTML, CSS, and JavaScript. Regardless of what happens between your computer (the client) and the computer that is holding the information about that page (the server), those three technologies are what the browser combines to get the job done and deliver the content to the screen (text, images, video, or animation).

Web pages are a little closer to the code than most designers are used to. Unlike Photoshop and Illustrator, where the code is never seen, with a Web page we can get in and play around with it, which is exactly what we will need to do if we want to get the exact visual results we desire.

CHAPTER 1

WHAT IS A WEB PAGE?

HTML, JavaScript, and CSS

It doesn't matter whether your Web pages are created using .ASP, PHP, MySQL, Python, Java, or any other of a multitude of available server-side technologies; when the pixel hits the screen on the browser side, you can be guaranteed that the browser is using one or all of these three core Web technologies to show it to you:

HTML provides structure, telling the browser what each element on the page is. HTML "tags" each piece of content, specifying whether it's a headline, a paragraph of text, an image, a table, a list, and so on. HTML does not actually tell the browser how those elements should look; it only defines what they are.

CSS provides presentation, telling the browser how each element should appear on the screen. CSS provides control over color, typography, sizes, and layout—whether an element is blue or brown, helvetica or arial—everything that goes into visually displaying the page.

JavaScript provides functionality, allowing the page to interact with the user and change after it has loaded. JavaScript lets you program the page, allowing everything from simple drop-down menus to full-blown Web-enabled apps.

Speaking in Styles

speaking-in-styles.com

Speaking in styles is more than just a book. Use the Web site to find updates, new ideas, and news about Web design.

HTML

Structure

CSS

Presentation

Functionality

JavaScript

HTML, JavaScript, and CSS continued

What Is the DOM?

A Web page document is a collection of different objects created using HTML and represented by something called the Document Object Model (DOM). DOM sounds kind of "techy," but really a *model* is simply a representation of something, an *object* is a part of that something, and the *document* is the something being represented. So, the DOM is a model of all the elements that make up your Web page, like a map to all the different pieces. Like a map, the DOM is not the page itself, but a way of representing the page so that we can think about its structure.

Each of the three core Web technologies has its own role to play in that map:

HTML defines objects, with each HTML tag creating a new unique object on the page that CSS can then style and JavaScript can change. For example, a header is an object, a paragraph is an object, and an image is an object.

CSS styles the objects, hooking into the HTML tags to style them individually or as a group and give each object a unique name called an ID.

JavaScript changes the objects, allowing you to make style and other changes to any object created with an HTML tag. For example, we can show an object, hide an object, or change the color of an object.

What About Flash?

There is one other technology that a lot of Web pages use to render content, and that's Adobe Flash. Pages built with Flash use a browser plug-in to render .fla files. Behind the scenes, though, Flash files are inserted into a page using HTML and can use CSS for style. We will talk about Flash throughout the book, and how it can play nicely with CSS, but primarily we will focus on the other core Web technologies.

HTML

Defines Objects

CSS

Styles Objects

DOM
Document Object Model

Changes Objects

JavaScript

HTML and CSS

The Hypertext Markup Language (HTML) structures your Web page by placing tags—small bits of code—around the different elements to tell the browser what a particular chunk of content is. CSS can then tell the browser what each of those chunks of content look like.

The different elements in the page are simply tagged to indicate their function: paragraphs are tagged with *<p>...</p>*, tables with *<table>...</table>*, list elements with *<li>...</li>*, and page headers with *<h1>...</h1>*. Most HTML code will tag the beginning of an element with an open tag and the end of an element with a close tag. So, a typical header will look like this:

<h1>Welcome</h1>

Browser-Inherent Styles

Although CSS should be used to add styles to the page, you will notice that HTML tags also add their own styles. For example, the level-1 header tag not only adds returns above and below, but also makes the text bolder and larger. There is no mystical law of the universe that says that header tags will be bolder and larger. No, it was the browser maker who programmed those styles to be inherently associated with that tag. Most HTML tags have some inherent or default styles associated with them. However, CSS allows you to change any of those browser-inherent styles with styles of your own.

As you would expect, a header puts a hard return above and below to set itself apart from other elements on the page. This is called a *block element*. Now that an element has been defined on the page, CSS can come along and tell the header exactly what it should look like: what font family to use, what color the text should be, its margins, border, padding, size, and other attributes. If we wanted the text to be a red, we might add code like this:

h1 { color: red; }

We could even tell the header to suppress the hard return above and below, turning it into an *inline element*.

HTML

<h1> Welcome</h1>

{ speaking in styles }

A CSS PRIMER *for* WEB DESIGNERS

Speaking In Styles is the forthcoming book by Jason Cranford Teague to help designers better understand how they can use CSS to create their designs for the Web.

More About *Speaking In Styles* →

Cover Concept

Jason Interviewed on Peachpit TV
Posted on *February 19th, 2009* by jason

Read more →

WHERE I'M SPEAKING...

SxSW Interactive
Austin, Tx | Online Comics & a reading from *Speaking in Styles.*
17 Mar 2009 03:30 PM | more +

Voices That Matter
San Francisco, Ca | Web Typography and Designing Credibility. Use the code **WBASPKR** to get a $200 discount.
27 Apr 2009 | more +

WHAT I'M DOING...

Just In: I'm going to be reading from my forth coming book _Speaking In Styles_ @SxSW (#SXO9-4648)
http://tinyurl.com/bivfb3 5 hrs ago

Whovians rejoice! Acclaimed Doctor Who author Simon Guerrier is now twittering under

PAGES

Contact
Inspirations
The Author
The Book

RECENT POSTS

Jason interviewed on Peachpit TV
Transparent PNGs (Yes, Even in IE6)
Jason interviewed by WOW
Browser Safe Fonts: Beta Available!
See You at Voices That Matter

CATEGORIES

Conferences (3)
Future (1)
Internet (1)
Typography (4)
Web Graphics (1)

h1 { color : red; }

CSS

CSS Genesis

In the early 1990s, a man named Tim Berners-Lee developed the Hypertext Markup Language (HTML), which let him display his research papers on the Internet with basic styles, such as underline, bold, and italic, and link these documents into a kind of "web" of documents. At first, all he wanted was to be able to display text and link relevant content together, but it quickly became necessary to show charts, graphs, and photos, so the ability to embed images in the page was added in the first graphics-based browser, Mosaic.

Originally, tags were used in HTML documents not only to structure the document, but to add the styles—so you had bold tags (<*b*>...</*b*>) and italics tags (<*i*>...</*i*>) and so forth. This meant the styles were locked into the structure, making design changes difficult.

More and more tags were added to deal with styling documents, but it was quickly realized that having the styles and the structure together was unworkable. Håkon Wium Lie and Bert Bos proposed using an existing technology called style sheets to allow designers to control how the HTML tags are styled. Thus CSS was born.

AllofUs

allofus.com

Design consultants AllofUs use HTML with a little CSS to create a simple but elegant design for their portfolio.

JavaScript and CSS

JavaScript adds interactivity to your Web page, through a script that tells the browser what to do when a particular action takes place. CSS sets the initial appearances on the page, which JavaScript can then change.

The scripts are used mostly to control elements on the page as the user interacts with them—showing menus, checking that form data has been entered correctly, and that sort of thing. But the capabilities of JavaScript have grown over the years so that it is now possible to create full-blown Web-enabled applications.

JavaScript works through the DOM to control the elements on the screen (created by the HTML tags) by changing the CSS values. For example, we might set the color of level-1 headers (*<h1>...</h1>*) to be a red:

h1 { color: rgb(255,0,0);}

Many sites allow users to choose the color scheme they see while at the site. One way to make this change would be to use JavaScript to dynamically change the color property:

object.style.color=rgb(153,51,41);

In this code, the variable *object* stands in for the object we want to make style changes to. It is derived from the DOM path to the *<h1>* tags. The full JavaScript code for finding the object would be something like:

object=document.getElementByTagName('h1');

This tells the JavaScript to find the header level-1 tags in the document so that we can make changes to their styles. There are many ways to find the objects on the page to make changes to them, but this is a book about CSS, not JavaScript, so we'll leave it at that for now.

h1 { color: rgb(255,0,0); }

{ speaking in styles }

A CSS PRIMER *for* WEB DESIGNERS

Welcome

Speaking In Styles is the forthcoming book by Jason Cranford Teague to help designers better understand how they can use CSS to create their designs for the Web.

More About *Speaking In Styles →*

Jason Interviewed on Peachpit TV
Posted on *February 19th, 2009 by Jason*

Read more →

Cover Concept

WHERE I'M SPEAKING...

SxSW Interactive
Austin, Tx | Online Comics & a reading from *Speaking In Styles.*
17 Mar 2009-03:30 PM | more -

Voices That Matter
San Francisco, Ca | Web Typography and Designing Credibility. Use the code **WBASPKR** to get a $200 discount.
27 Apr 2009 | more -

WHAT I'M DOING...

Just in: I'm going to be reading from my forth coming book _Speaking in Styles_ @SxSW (#SX09-4648)
http://tinyurl.com/blvfb3 5 hrs ago

Whovians rejoice! Acclaimed Doctor Who author Simon Guerrier is now twittering under

PAGES
Contact
Inspirations
The Author
The Book

RECENT POSTS
Jason Interviewed on Peachpit TV
Transparent PNGs (Yes, Even in IE6)
Jason Interviewed by WOW
Browser Safe Fonts: Beta Available!
See You at Voices That Matter

CATEGORIES
Conferences (3)
Future (1)
Internet (1)
Typography (4)
Web Graphics (1)

object.style.color=rgb(153,51,41)

Know Your Code: JavaScript

Generally speaking, designers rarely have to look at, much less create, JavaScript. That said, it will be extremely useful to have at least a passing knowledge of what JavaScript is capable of doing, as well as knowing the names of some of JavaScript's popular offshoots and flavors, especially if you plan on doing any type of user experience work:

Dynamic HTML, or *DHTML*, refers to JavaScript used to control HTML and CSS after the page has loaded. This can include making style changes, dynamic elements like menus and pop-ups, and special effects such as fades and slides.

Asynchronous JavaScript and XML, or *Ajax*, uses JavaScript to pass information back and forth between the loaded Web page and the server without having to reload the entire page. This allows the user to interact with large amounts of data without having to load it all up front.

JavaScript Object Notation, or *JSON* (yes, it's pronounced like my name, but I had nothing to do with it) is a quick and easy way for JavaScript to transfer data that's easier to use and understand than alternatives like XML.

MooTools, jQuery, and *Dojo Toolkit* are all popular JavaScript libraries that provide ready-built functionality that takes a lot of the grunt work out of creating controls and effects such as dynamic menus, calendars, fades, and animations. Although there is some overlap, each library has its own strengths and weaknesses, and each has its loyal followers in the Web dev community. Another benefit to these libraries is that they eliminate a lot of cross-browser headaches associated with JavaScript. If you are developing your own Web site, I recommend checking these libraries out and putting them to use.

Krista's Creations at Letter-Photo

letter-photo.com

Using a simple drag-and-drop interface created with JavaScript and CSS, Krista's Creations allows you to create cool signs out of photographed letters and letter-like shapes and then order prints.

Flash and CSS

Although no one seems to talk about it much, CSS can be applied to Flash files to control their appearance. So, there are a mess of caveats— for example, it's only used for styling text and you have to use ActionScript to load the external CSS file—but it is doable.

Just like CSS with HTML, using CSS with Flash can save you a lot of time when your client tells you two days before the site is supposed to launch that they don't want to use green hypertext links because green is an unlucky color (yes, this has happened to me). Without CSS, Flash will embed styles directly into the .swf file, making them difficult to change on a large scale. Imagine trying to change all of your link colors if you had to open dozens of individual Flash files! With CSS, you can change a single line of code to update your entire site to the new color.

Where the CSS/Flash partnership will really shine, though, is when you style XML formatted data. Since XML allows you to, in effect, create your own "tags," CSS is a natural to style these tags.

Causecast

causecast.com

The Social-networking site Causecast uses Flash to both deliver its video and for the interface to interact with that video. However, the rest of the site uses HTML, CSS, and JavaScript.

welcome to panic®

drag any app here to instantly download:

what's the latest?

Noby Noby
Boy shirts!

applications

① ABOUT
emails, contact

GOODS
wonderful t-shirts

◉ EXTRAS
apps, culture, etc

© 2007 PANIC INC. PANIC, THE PANIC LOGO, AND TRANSMIT ARE REGISTERED TRADEMARKS OF PANIC INC.

パニック・ジャパン トップページ

All artists have a tool set that they know and rely upon. Sculptors choose the best chisels; painters choose the best brushes; calligraphers choose the best pens. Likewise, Web designers need to choose the best tools at their disposal not only to visualize their designs but to also create them in their medium of choice, the Web browser. The tools you choose will not make you a better designer, but they can help you make better designs.

CHAPTER 2

WEB DESIGNER'S TOOLBOX

Web Browsers

What browser do you use to surf the Web? Some people have a favorite browser. Some choose based on their job. Others simply use the default browser on their machine and may never be aware that other options exist. Regardless of your personal preference, however, your designs will need to work on all of the most common browsers. To compound the issue, when a new version of a browser is released, older versions do not magically disappear (IF ONLY!), so you also have to test on *legacy* browsers.

Microsoft's Internet Explorer is inarguably the most commonly used Web browser, with a market share of about 70% of the Web viewing public. The exact number will vary depending on location and audience, though. For example, designers have a higher percentage of Mac users than other audiences, and the Mac does not include a recent version of Internet Explorer. So, that audience tends more toward Safari or Firefox.

All modern browsers support CSS; however, not all browsers do so equally. Throughout this book, I'll point out where browsers do not have or are deficient in the particular features I'm discussing. First, let's get a quick overview of the four most common browsers you will encounter.

Panic Software

panic.com

Panic Software is a purveyor of fine Web tools.

Browser Differences

The same Web page displayed in four different browsers: IE6, FF3, Sa4, and Op9. The obvious stand out is IE6, which will take some rethinking of the code to get it working properly. The good news is that IE7 fixes many of these issues.

Web Browsers continued

Internet Explorer (IE)

Windows

microsoft.com/ie

For a while, Internet Explorer overwhelmingly dominated the Web browser market, rising to as high as a 90% market share at times. Unfortunately, IE6 had several flaws when its came to it implementation of CSS, including the exclusion of several important features and the misinterpretation of others. Although IE7 has gone a long way in adopting CSS standards, it still has several issues, and, of course, IE6 is still out there. The good news is that the IE6 market share has rapidly fallen and is now at around 15–20% globally, and IE8 fully embraces the current version of CSS (v2.1).

Firefox (FF)

Mac, Windows, and Unix/Linux

firefox.com

In general, I recommend starting your development by testing in Firefox. It has a strong implementation of the current CSS standards (v2.1), includes many future CSS standards (v3.0), is the second most widely used Web browser (22% of market share), and it allows you to install add-ons that help with coding CSS. If your design works in Firefox, then it will work almost the same in both Safari and Opera, and most likely in IE7 and IE8. IE6, on the other hand, will take a bit of work.

Safari (Sa)

Mac and Windows

apple.com/safari

Many designers will develop in Safari, since it is the default browser on all Macs. Sa4 has, arguably, the best implementation of the CSS standards so far. This implementation not only includes all current standards (v2.1), but also many still in development (v3.0) and a few styles of its own. This is a mixed blessing, since it can mean you are using styles or features that are not currently available in other browsers.

Opera (Op)

Mac, Windows, and Unix

opera.com

Often overlooked, Opera is more popular than you might realize. It is used in many European mobile devices as well as on Sony's PlayStation gaming system. Op9 equals Sa3 in CSS standards compliance but does not have some of the advanced features. If you don't have the most recent version of Opera, get with the downloading. Like all of the best things in life, it's free!

Web Browsers continued

Test Internet Explorer 6 on the Mac with Crossover

codeweavers.com/products/cxmac

One of the hardest issues to deal with on the Mac is how to test your designs in IE6, which is still very popular and only available for Windows. One great and inexpensive solution is a program called Crossover, which allows you to run many Windows applications directly on your Mac desktop without having to own or install Windows on your machine. Currently, it does not support IE 7 or 8, which is a shame, but these two browsers have fewer page-rendering inconsistencies than their predecessor.

Other Browsers Do Exist!

Although more than 99.3% of people surfing the Web today are using one of the four browsers listed here, dozens of other browsers are often popular with niche markets. But don't panic! Almost all of them are based on the same layout engines as Internet Explorer, Firefox, Safari, or Opera, so they should render your pages the same way. Check the layout engines table on the next page to see which of the more popular alternative browsers are roughly equivalent.

Layout Engines:
The Power Under the Browser Hood

Think of a browser like it's a car: What you see is just the shell around the engine, which is what makes the car move. You can take the engine out of one car and put it in another—even a different model. Browsers have *layout engines* (also called *rendering engines*) that drive how the browser displays Web pages. Although there are different layout engines, many browsers use the same engine, but with a different interface around it.

For example, Firefox uses the open-source rendering engine Gecko, and so does Camino, Netscape, and Flock. They each add their own user interface on top, though. All browsers using the same rendering engine will all display Web pages about the same way. There may be slight variations, depending on which version of the rendering engine was used and whether any tweaks were made to it—just like a car engine that has been tuned for a particular car.

Engine Name	Browsers
Gecko	Firefox, Camino, Netscape, Flock
Trident	Internet Explorer, AOL Explorer, MSN Explorer, RealPlayer
KHTML and WebKit	Safari, Google Chrome, Shiira, OmniWeb, iCab, Konquerer
Presto	Opera, Nintendo DS Browser, Internet Channel (Wii)
Java	Lobo, Opera Mini

Firefox Add-Ons

Firefox makes a great development browser, not only because it has strong standards compliance, is available for Mac, Windows, and Unix/Linux, and is the second most commonly used browser, but also because you can install a variety of add-ons, small programs that run within the browser, to enhance its capabilities. Here are a few of my favorites:

Firebug

addons.mozilla.org/firefox/1843

Firebug is an indispensable tool for anyone creating a Web site in Firefox. It enables you to:

» View and edit the HTML, CSS, and JavaScript code of the page being displayed and edit it on the fly.

» Identify any element on the page, showing you all of its full context and any styles applied to it.

» View the Web page as it loads to see how long each element takes to download, letting you identify any bottlenecks in your design.

Colorzilla

addons.mozilla.org/firefox/271

Allows you to sample the color of any pixels in the Web browser, displaying the value in both hex and RGB values. Simply choose the eyedropper, then click a pixel. You can then copy and paste the color code into another application as needed.

Selected element

HTML code   CSS code

Firebug for Firefox

With Firebug, you can inspect the HTML and
CSS code used to create any element on the
page, and even edit the code on the fly to test
out different ideas.

Firefox Add-Ons continued

Palette Grabber

addons.mozilla.org/firefox/2290

Grab all of the color values out of a Web site's CSS and turn them into a working color palette for Photoshop and other programs with Palette Grabber. All it takes is a single click to save a palette, then you can load it into your favorite image editing software to start working.

MeasureIt

addons.mozilla.org/firefox/539

Have you ever had something on the screen and you needed to find its size? Or noticed that the alignment of two objects wasn't quite right but weren't sure by how much? Then MeasureIt is the tool for you. You click an icon, select the area width and height you want to measure, and MeasureIt displays the dimensions in pixels, taking out a lot of the guesswork when precision is your goal.

Pixel Perfect

addons.mozilla.org/firefox/7943

If you like your sites to look exactly like your visual comps, you'll need Pixel Perfect. This is actually an add-on to Firebug (an add-on to an add-on) that allows you to load a a JPEG version of your visual comp as an onion skin over the top of the live version to compare your vision to the reality on the Web.

Firefox Add-Ons

addons.mozilla.org

You can spend hours surfing around and trying out different Firefox add-ons. If you need something, there's probably an add-on for it.

Code Editors

Just as you have a word processor for writing or an illustration program for drawing, you need a Web development program for coding. A good code editor will:

» Organize and edit documents, providing suggestions where needed.

» Preview documents without having to jump between multiple browsers.

» Download and upload documents as you work on them.

» Analyze and optimize your code.

Coda

Mac

panic.com/coda/

Coda is my program of choice whenever I edit code. Coda (Panic Software) includes integrated FTP, making uploading and downloading files a breeze. Its CSS editing tools allow you to get straight at the code or to use a more designer-friendly visual interface.

TopStyle

Windows

newsgator.com/individuals/topstyle

Although I generally recommend designing on a Mac, if you are using a PC running Windows, TopStyle is similar to Coda.

CSSEdit

Mac

macrabbit.com/cssedit/

If you are a designer who is only interested in working with CSS code (and not HTML or JavaScript), CSSEdit has everything you need. It includes some impressive tools for analyzing the CSS of an existing Web site.

Dreamweaver

Windows and Mac

adobe.com/dreamweaver

Dreamweaver, which comes with many Adobe software packages, is often the default choice for designers. Of all of the code editors, Dreamweaver is possibly the most feature rich, but it is also the most expensive, and more features also means it's harder to learn to use.

Online Tools

We typically think of an application as something that you get on a disk or download and then install onto your computer. Increasingly, applications are being delivered through the Web, without requiring you to install or download the specific application. Some of the best tools in my arsenal aren't on my desktop; they're online. The line between Web *site* and Web *application* (or just *Web app*) is gradually being blurred. Like you do with a Web site, you get to a Web app by using a Web browser and URL, but Web apps provide functionality like you would expect from a traditional application.

ColorJack

colorjack.com

Adobe Kuler

kuler.adobe.com

Every designer has to deal with color. It can be difficult to define a palette of colors that work well together but provide the spectrum needed. ColorJack and Adobe Kuler are Web apps that allow you to put together a color palette, helping you choose the best combinations based on color theory. You can then save the results for use in common image editing software such as Photoshop and Illustrator.

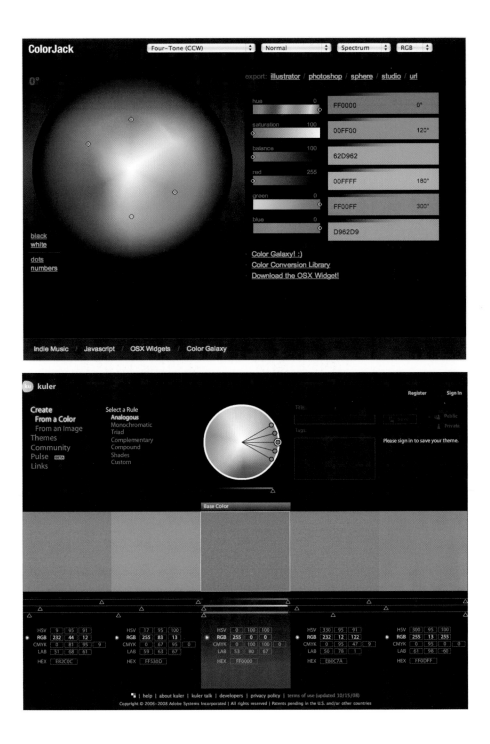

Online Tools continued

Typetester

typetester.org

Good typography on the Web seems like an oxymoron, but it's getting better. Typetester allows you to preview how different font families will look at various sizes, weights, and styles. Just choose from an extensive list of Web-safe fonts or from a list of fonts installed on your computer, and the results are instantly displayed underneath.

SUMO Paint

sumopaint.com

If you are a designer, you likely already have an image editor of choice like Photoshop, Fireworks, or Illustrator. These applications can be costly, but free alternatives are available on the Web. SUMO Paint allows you to create and edit layered bitmap images in a familiar Photoshop-like interface. If you are strapped for cash, it may just be what youare looking for. Although limited in its feature set, it has all of the basic tools you would need to put together simple Web graphics.

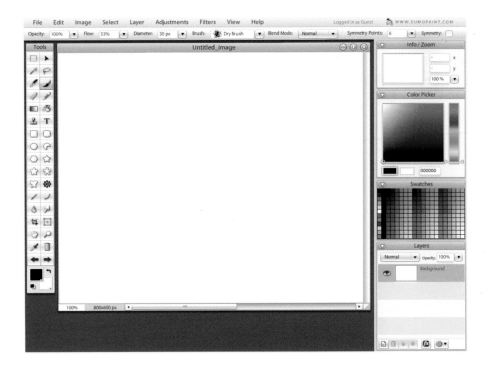

N/A Subscribers

HOME   ABOUT   JOBS

Search

FEB
23

▾ Design Trends, Inspiration

50 Minimal Sites

108

Since Web Designer Wall launched, I've been featuring a lot of graphic intense websites such as the artistic, large background, vintage, and illustrative styles. Now it is time to feature the minimalist design. Here is a massive list of 50 minimal sites. See how designers use minimal elements to create high visual impact — *less is more.*

Add to → ▪ Delicious   Stumbleupon   Digg

FEB
21

▾ Updates

Launch: IconDock

67

Folks! I'm very excited to annouce the launch of my new site — IconDock. It is a icon shop where I sell stock icons and offer free icons for download. The main focus of IconDock is to provide vector icons that you can use for print and web design. You can buy icons individually or a complete set. Even if you are not interested in buying the icons, check out the site anyway to see the Ajax-powered shop with drag & drop features.

Add to → ▪ Delicious   Stumbleupon   Digg

FEB
18

▾ Event, Freebies

Free FITC Tickets (Round 1)

160

Have you heard of **FITC** (this is their 8th year)? Do you want to get a free ticket to attend this upcoming event in Toronto between April 25 - 28, 2009? For those who don't know what is FITC, it is a design conference filled with **presentations** (read **details**). This year WDW is one of their media supporters. As usually, I have free tickets to give out (6 in total). From now to April, I will give out 2 tickets per month. Enter your comment in this post for your chance to win a free ticket.

If you would like to purchase the tickets, enter coupon code "webdesignerwall" to get a 20% discount.

Add to → ▪ Delicious   Stumbleupon   Digg

FEB
12

▾ Design, Design Process

Dache: Logo Design Process

76

Previously, I have featured **David Pache** of **Dache** on WDW, an amazing logo designer from Switzerland. He is known for designing unique and colorful logos. I'm very glad to have David to share his design process of the WebMYnd's logo. This case study (written by David himself) provides full creative brief and progress images from start to final. Read on to find out how David got inspired by **Wassily Kandinsky**'s art (one of the most famous 20th-century abstract artists) to create this fantastic logo.

WebMynd

Add to → ▪ Delicious   Stumbleupon   Digg

FEB
09

▾ CSS, Javascript

jQuery Sequential List

56

Have you ever had to manually code something that is sequential? Didn't you find it annoning?

▸ TUTORIALS
how to, css, photoshop...

▸ TRENDS
inspiration, web trends...

▸ GENERAL
news, technology, etc.

TAG CLOUD

CSS Design
Design Process
Design Trends Event Flash
Freebies Illustrator
Inspiration Javascript
Jobs
Photoshop Tutorials
Review SEO Software
Talented People Updates
WordPress

Ads

DESIGN JOBS
— on the Wall

★ Designer / Programmer
at GearSource, Inc (Florida or Calgary, Alberta)

★ Front End Web Designer/Developer
at Millennium Communications (Syosset, NY)

★ Web Developer / Designer with UI and SEO Experience
at Edvisors (Boston (Quincy) Ma)

★ Looking for top-tier web designer
at DNA 11 (Anywhere)

Over the years, many different myths and misconceptions have grown up around Cascading Style Sheets—some good and some bad. You may have heard some of these myths and may still believe them: CSS is computer code; CSS is buggy; CSS is only for styling type and color. Some of these myths were never true, others are no longer true, and some have a grain of truth. Before we go any further into learning how to speak in styles, let's clear the air about three of the most persistent CSS myths.

Chapter 3

The Myths of CSS

Myth 1:
CSS Is for Developers, Not Designers

False: Many designers coming to CSS for the first time think that it's just for the "coders" and not for "real" designers. I hear this a lot from designers: "I don't want to learn to program a computer." Designers who buy this line of reasoning have three basic arguments:

Argument 1: *If the developers understand it, then I don't need to.* I started my design life as a print designer, and I had to understand the print process from beginning to end. I had to know about CMYK, paper weights, register marks, and how to create files for output. I had to understand these things, not because I was going to run one of those massive Koenig & Bauer printing presses, but because I wanted to get the best results from my designs in my selected medium. At the very least, even if you never plan to touch the code yourself, understanding how CSS works will make you a better Web designer.

Argument 2: *CSS is too hard to learn.* CSS was actually developed with designers in mind. Natural language terms are used wherever possible to make it easy to understand and remember.

Argument 3: *I'm a designer, damn it, not a programmer.* CSS is a *style sheet language*, not a *programming language*. What's the difference? Style sheet languages are used to simply tell the computer how the different objects in a document should be presented, using simple style rules that humans can easily understand rather than logic-based functions. CSS is used to describe how the content should appear, not how it should work.

WebDesignerWall

webdesignerwall.com

If you are looking for innovative Web design ideas from designers, using CSS, take a look at the Web Designer Wall.

MYTH

CSS is for Web Developers, Not Web Designers

CSS is a

style language

anyone can learn to
read and write.

TRUTH

Design Shack's CSS Gallery

designshack.co.uk/gallery/

Numerous Web sites highlight great designer
portfolios created using CSS.

Web Designer Michela Chiucini

colazionedamichy.it

Designer Michela Chiucini uses CSS with WordPress to create her own portfolio and gives away a few templates for you to start using.

Myth 2:
CSS Can't Handle the Designs I Need

False: Design is about overcoming the limits of your medium. All media have different strengths and weaknesses, and Web design with CSS is no different. CSS can handle a wide variety of different designs, and the more you know about its limitations, the better you can design to its strengths.

Most designers who believe the myth that CSS can't handle a variety of layouts are usually from the old school of Web design, when the only option for creating a grid-based layout was by using HTML tables. Yes, tables can do some things that CSS still cannot do—like creating balanced column heights, although that will be possible in the future— but the advantages of designing with CSS far outweigh the advantages of table-based layout. The techniques that designers use today are vastly different from those we used just a few years ago. As we've had a chance to explore the capabilities of CSS, new ideas and new methods are constantly being explored.

There is no better example of the versatility of CSS than the CSS Zen Garden. This simple site is a single Web page, which you can download the HTML code for and create your own CSS design solution. Over 200 designers have taken the challenge, with more coming all the time. Each design is completely different from the others, but all use the exact same HTML code as their basis. With tables, which lock the structure directly into the HTML, this versatility is lost.

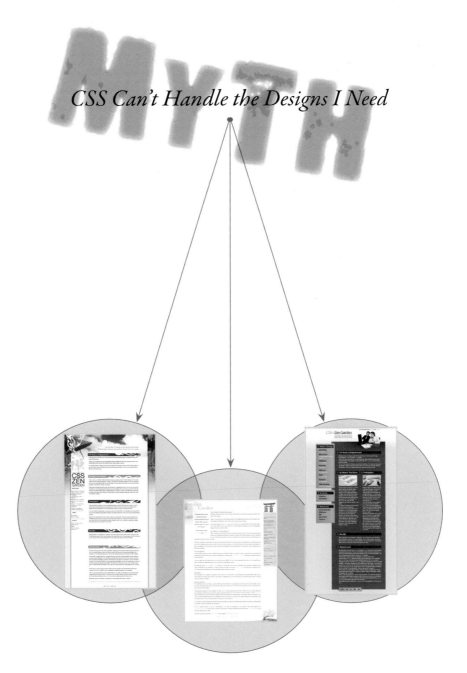

CSS Can't Handle the Designs I Need

MYTH

TRUTH

Zen Garden

The Beauty of CSS Design

The Road to Enlightenment

A demonstration of what can be accomplished visually through CSS-based design. Select any style sheet from the list to load it into this page.

Download the sample html file and css file

Littering a dark and dreary road lay the past relics of browser-specific tags, incompatible DOMs, and broken CSS support.

Today, we must clear the mind of past practices. Web enlightenment has been achieved thanks to the tireless efforts of folk like the W3C, WaSP and the major browser creators.

The css Zen Garden invites you to relax and meditate on the important lessons of the masters. Begin to see with clarity. Learn to use the (yet to be) time-honored techniques in new and invigorating fashion. Become one with the web.

So What is This About?

There is clearly a need for CSS to be taken seriously by graphic artists. The Zen Garden aims to excite, inspire, and encourage participation. To begin, view some of the existing designs in the list. Clicking on any one will load the style sheet into this very page. The code remains the same, the only thing that has changed is the external .css file. Yes, really.

CSS allows complete and total control over the style of a hypertext document. The only way this can be illustrated in a way that gets people excited is by demonstrating what it can truly be, once the reins are placed in the hands of those able to create beauty from structure. To date, most examples of neat tricks and hacks have been demonstrated by structurists and coders. Designers have yet to make their mark. This needs to change.

Participation

Graphic artists only please. You are modifying this page, so strong CSS skills are necessary, but the example files are commented well enough that even CSS novices can use them as starting points. Please see the CSS Resource Guide for advanced tutorials and tips on working with CSS.

You may modify the style sheet in any way you wish, but not the HTML. This may seem daunting at first if you've never worked this way before, but follow the listed links to learn more, and use the sample files as a guide.

Download the sample html file and css file to work on a copy locally. Once you have completed your masterpiece (and please, don't submit half-finished work) upload your .css file to a web server under your control. Send us a link to the file and if we choose to use it, we will spider the associated images. Final submissions will be placed on our server.

Benefits

Why participate? For recognition, inspiration, and a resource we can all refer to when making the case for CSS-based design. This is sorely needed, even today. More and more major sites are taking the leap, but not enough have. One day this gallery will be a historical curiosity; that day is not today.

Requirements

We would like to see as much CSS1 as possible. CSS2 should be limited to widely-supported elements only. The css Zen Garden is about functional, practical CSS and not the latest bleeding-edge tricks viewable by 2% of the browsing public. The only real requirement we have is that your CSS validates.

Unfortunately, designing this way highlights the flaws in the various implementations of CSS. Different browsers display differently, even completely valid CSS at times, and this becomes maddening when a fix for one leads to breakage in another. View the Resources page for information on some of the fixes available. Full browser compliance is still sometimes a pipe dream, and we do not expect you to come up with pixel-perfect code across every platform. But do test in as many as you can. If your design doesn't work in at least IE5+/Win and Mozilla (run by over 90% of the population), chances are we won't accept it.

We ask that you submit original artwork. Please respect copyright laws. Please keep objectionable material to a minimum; tasteful nudity is acceptable, outright pornography will be rejected.

This is a learning exercise as well as a demonstration. You retain full copyright on your graphics (with limited exceptions, see submission guidelines), but we ask you release your CSS under a Creative Commons license identical to the one on this site so that others may learn from your work.

Bandwidth graciously donated by mediatemple. Now available: Zen Garden, the book.

xhtml   css   cc   508   aaa

select a design:

Under the Seal by Eric Stoltz

Make 'em Proud by Michael McAghon and Scotty Reifsnyder

Orchid Beauty by Kevin Addison

Oceanscape by Justin Gray

CSS Co., Ltd. by Benjamin Klemm

Sakura by Tatsuya Uchida

Kyoto Forest by John Politowski

A Walk in the Garden by Simon Van Hauwermeiren

archives:

next designs »

View All Designs

resources:

View This Design's CSS

CSS Resources

FAQ

Submit a Design

Translations

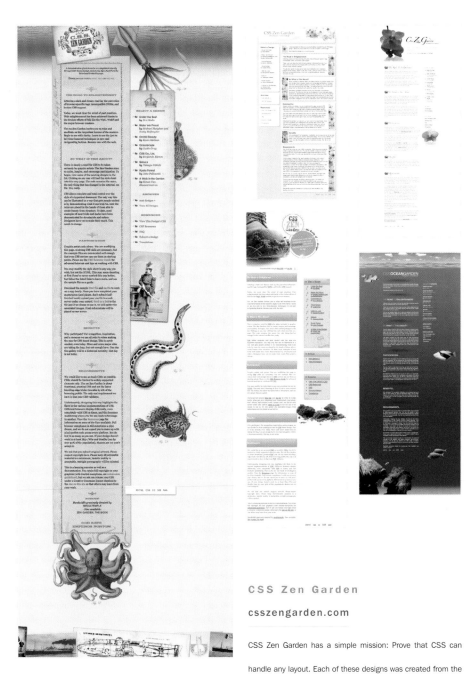

CSS Zen Garden

csszengarden.com

CSS Zen Garden has a simple mission: Prove that CSS can

handle any layout. Each of these designs was created from the

same HTML code but with different CSS styling it.

Myth 3:
CSS Has Too Many Browser Inconsistencies

Mostly **False**: OK, so there's some truth to this particular myth, but it's not as bad as you might think. CSS is a standard, which means that an organization—the World Wide Web Consortium (W3C)—has set up some very specific instructions on how it should work. The problem is, like all human communication, instructions are open to interpretation (or can just be ignored) by the browser makers. Mozilla, Opera, Apple, and Microsoft are the main players in the field.

Every browser has its own quirks when it comes to CSS, but it's Microsoft's Internet Explorer that deviates the most from the straight and narrow path of Web standards.

For many years, most of the problems were with Internet Explorer—specifically IE6. The issues with IE6 are legendary, and I will highlight them throughout this book with tips on overcoming them. While it used to be that a good quarter of your development time would be spent just trying to get your Web pages to look roughly the same in IE6 as in other browsers, most of the inconsistencies are now gone or easily circumvented. IE7, while far from perfect, is much closer to standards compliance than previous versions, and on the horizon is IE8, which promises even closer CSS adoption. IE 7 is now the most popular Web browser in use, while IE6 quickly evaporates in popularity.

That doesn't mean you can ignore the older versions, but you do not always have to provide the same experience. Instead, designers will create a usable but stripped-down design for IE6. The design still works just fine; it just may not have all of the design bells and whistles.

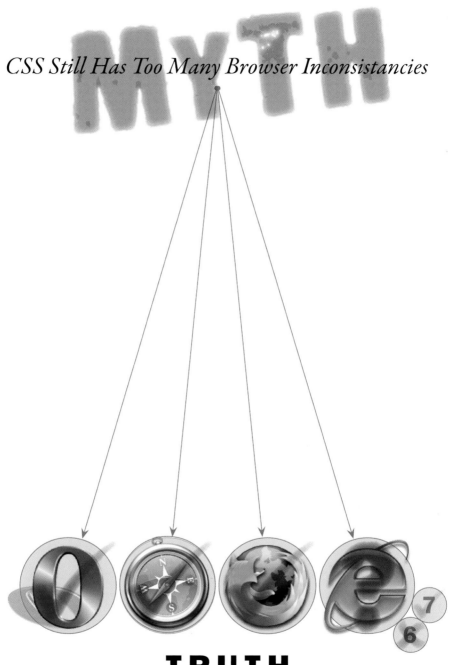

CSS Still Has Too Many Browser Inconsistancies

TRUTH

PART 2

In which the reader learns the syntax (how the language is put together), semantics (how the language is understood), and vocabulary (the words used in the language) that make up the grammar of CSS.

CSS Grammar

UGSMAG

Search

💬 13   *Interview*

Selfhelp

Seven years after the Bending Mouth project with Thesis Sahib, Selfhelp is now living in Saskatchewan and back with an impressive debut solo album, 'Old Friends'.

Read more

News

>> Submit N

May 10   💬 6   Vi

Ceschi - "Black & White & Red All Over" live video

Awesome video of Ceschi performing an accoustic version of "Black & White & Red All Over".

May 10   💬 7   Au

ira lee - "I Love My Mom"

I ♥ MOM

To celebrate Mother's day ira lee and Swiss/German producer Mattr have teamed up to bring you a free download.

May 9   💬 1   *Album Downlo*

BIG TReaL - Stimulus EP

BIG TREAL
The Stimulus Package

Free download EP from Charlotte, North Carolina emcee BIG TReaL. The *Stimulus* EP features origina production from 9th Wonder Eric ...

May 9   💬 1   N

The Nope (Psy & Moka Only) "Rain All Day"

New digital single from The Nope (Psy of the Oddities and Moka Only). The single is taken from their upcomin album *Melba* to be released this Summer...

May 9   💬 Comment   Au

Breez Evahflowin - "Over"

First single from Breez Evahflowin's upcoming album *Breez Deez Treez* to be released this Summer or Domination Recordings.

Featured Articles

💬 27   *Interview*

soso & Dj Kutdown

Long time Canadian hip hop producers, soso and Dj Kutdown, recently collloborated their skills on an instrumental album.

💬 14   *Interview*

Dragon Fli Empire

Calgary rap duo Dragon Fli Empire (Teekay and Dj Cosm) chat about Canadian hip hop, their new album "Redefine" and much more.

💬 21   *Interview*

Pip Skid

We catch up with Pip Skid as he talks Peanuts & Corn, Marathon of Dope, new projects and more...

💬 36   *Features*

Conspiracy = The Ol' Dirty Bastard of C...

A heartfelt plea from his twin brother Mindbender.

💬 80   *Interview*

Cam the Wizzard

Cam the Wizzard is arguably the cameo king of Alberta rap. His latest project is a group with Factor and Subtitle.

💬 10   *Photo Mission*

King of the Dot: *Put Yo Money Where Yo Mo...*

A set of photos from the K.O.T.D. Put Yo Money Where Yo Mouth Iz Volume 5 battle in Toronto.

➕ Read More News
📶 RSS for Updates

Recent Comments

ira lee - "I Love My Mom" by workturkey
I like.

ira lee - "I Love My Mom" by epic
I like the jonny cash and June song

ira lee - "I Love My Mom" by epic

Newsletter

Subscribe to UGSMAG's monthly newsletter for contests, news and more.

Name

D-SISIVE

Syntax is how you put words together to create meaning: Punctuation and parts of speech are placed in a specific order to describe something. How you combine these elements has a direct effect on the meaning of what you are trying to communicate. To describe your Web designs, you need to understand the syntax of CSS.

Although CSS syntax is relatively simple compared to the syntax of a language such as English, it is also less forgiving of mistakes. A misplaced comma or semicolon might change your styles completely or might even turn your styles into incomprehensible gibberish, at least to the browser. But once you get the hang of it, you'll be speaking in CSS in no time.

CHAPTER 4

SYNTAX
CREATING MEANING

The Rules of Style

Web pages are created using HTML tags to add structure to the page. Most of these tags have inherent styles—that is, styles that the browser manufacturer has set as the default. If we left it to the browser to style our pages, they would all look pretty much the same, and none too interesting. CSS acts on the HTML tags telling them how they should appear when rendered on the screen. To change a tag's style, you create CSS rules that bind styles to particular elements on the screen, either directly to a specific HTML tag or using a class or ID that can then be applied to any HTML tag you desire.

Let's keep it simple for now, and start by looking at how we create a basic style for the header level 1 HTML tag *<h1>*. CSS rules begin with a selector, which is what is being defined, followed by a declaration or list of declarations between curly brackets to define the selector's style.

UGSMAG

ugsmag.com

Independent Canadian hip hop magazine UGSMAG speaks to its audience with a unique visual voice created with CSS.

Selector   Declaration

h1 { color: red; }

Curly Brackets

The Rules of Style continued

Parts of a Style Rule

A CSS rule has the equivalents of the subject, object, verb, and adjective that you would find in any English sentence:

- The *subject* (what we are describing) is the *selector*.

- The *object* (what is being described about the subject) is the *property*.

- The *verb* (always the verb "to be" in CSS) is represented by a *colon*.

- The *adjective* (the description) is the *value*.

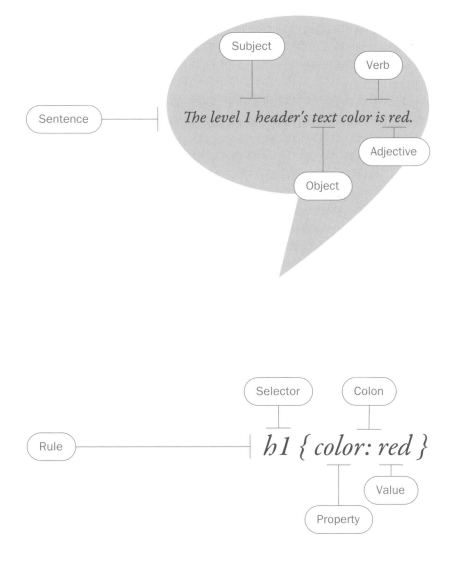

The Rules of Style continued

A Basic Style Rule

To tell another person that you want a level 1 header to be red, you might say something like:

The level 1 header's text color is red.

In CSS, to communicate the exact same thing, you could say:

h1 { color: red }

In this case, color refers to the text color and red is a predefined keyword that the browser translates into an actual color value. We could also use the RGB scale:

h1 { color: rgb(255,0,0) }

Or the hexadecimal color scale:

h1 { color: #ff0000 }

These all say the same thing: The first-level header's text color is red. In English this is called a declarative sentence. In CSS this is called a CSS rule or *selector declaration*.

You are declaring style properties for the selector, in this case the h1 selector, which effects the *<h1>* tag. There are three types of selectors in CSS. The one shown here is an HTML selector because it corresponds to a specific HTML tag. We will learn about class and ID selectors a bit later in this chapter.

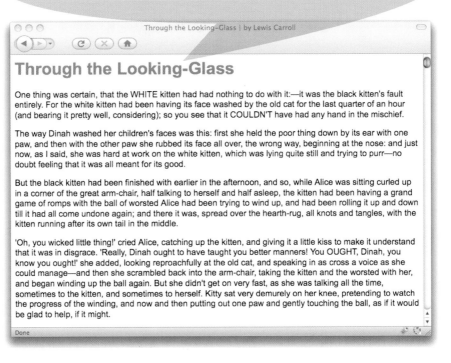

The level 1 header's text color is red.

<h1> Through the Looking-Glass </h1>

h1 { color : red }

h1 { color : rgb(255,0,0) }

h1 { color : #ff0000}

The Rules of Style continued

Declaring More Styles

To add multiple declarations to your rule, separate each by a semicolon. You can have one, two, ten, one hundred, or however many declarations you want in a single rule, as long as you separate each by a semicolon, just like you might use a comma or semicolon to separate the items in a sentence:

The level 1 header's color is red, the font family is Georgia, and the font size is 24px.

To say the same thing in CSS, you list the declarations:

h1 { color: red; font-family: Georgia; font-size: 24px; }

Notice that I've put a semicolon after each declaration, including the last one. In the previous example, where there was only one declaration, I didn't add a semicolon because you don't have to put a semicolon after the last declaration in a list; you could just leave it off. Now, forget you ever read that:

Always put a semicolon after every declaration in your list, even the last one.

Why? Because one day you will make a change to that CSS rule. You will add another declaration at the end of the list and you will forget to add the semicolon to the previous line, and your style will simply stop working. You will spend hours trying to figure out why your styles are not working only to discover it was because you forgot to add one stupid semicolon. How do I know this? I have spent far too many hours of my life banging my head against my keyboard trying to figure out why my styles aren't working, all because of a missing semicolon. Learn from my mistakes: Always include the semicolon after *every* declaration.

The level 1 header's text color is red, the font family is Georgia, and the font size is 24px.

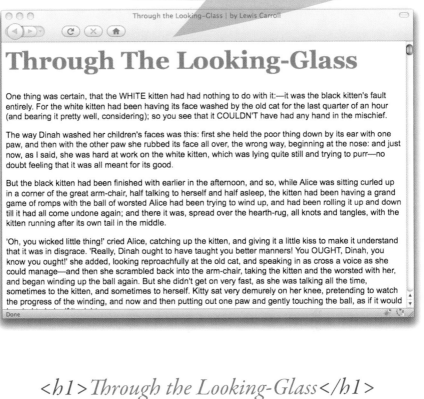

```
<h1>Through the Looking-Glass</h1>
```

```
h1 {
      color : red;
      font-family: Georgia;
      font-size: 24px;
}
```

Semicolons

The Rules of Style continued

Combining Rules

What happens when the same styles are being applied to different selectors? For example, what if you want all of your headers to be red? You could create three different style rules, one for each header level:

h1 { color: red; }   h2 { color: red; }   h3 { color: red; }

When speaking, though, you wouldn't say:

The level 1 header's text color is red.

The level 2 header's text color is red.

The level 3 header's text color is red.

Instead, you would combine these into a single sentence using commas:

The level 1, level 2, and level 3 header's text color is red.

Similarly, you can apply the same style declarations to multiple selectors in the same rule by putting them into a comma separated list:

h1, h2, h3 { color: red; }

Now the first three header levels will be red. Besides saving a lot of space, which is important once your CSS files start getting large, this also has the advantage of putting all of the selectors that use this value into a single place, making it easier to change later. For example, if your boss or client decides they want green headers instead of red, rather than changing the value in three places, you only have to change it once:

h1, h2, h3 { color: green; }

The level 1, level 2, and level 3 header's text color is red.

<h1> Through the Looking-Glass</h1>
<h3>By Lewis Carroll</h3>
<h2>CHAPTER I...</h2>

h1, h2, h3 { color : red; }

Commas

Types of Selectors

So far, you've only seen one kind of selector: the HTML selector. This allows you to specify how any HTML tag on the page should be styled. If all you could do was style HTML tags and all of the paragraphs looked the same, and all of the level 2 headers looked the same, and all of the lists looked the same, and so forth, your designs would look pretty boring. You need ways to selectively style HTML tags with CSS.

For example, you might have your level 2 headers look one way when in the main text of an article, another in the sidebar, and yet a third when used as the caption for a photo.

CSS provides three distinct selector types that enable you to tailor your design to appear exactly the way you want.

HTML Selector

To define how a particular HTML tag should be styled indiscriminately across your Web page, use its HTML selector. For example, if you say that all header level 2 tags should be red:

The level 2 header's text color is red.

h2 { color: red; }

The styles will be applied to any content tagged with:

<h2>...</h2>

All header level 2 tags on the page will be red, unless you override its declarations with other declarations. More about that later.

The level 2 header's text color is red.

HTML Selector

h2 { color : red; }

<h2> Chapter I...</h2>
<h2> Chapter II...</h2>
<h2> Chapter III...</h2>

h2 { color : red; }

<h2> Chapter I</h2>
<h2>Chapter II</h2>
<h2>Chapter III</h2>

CHAPTER I. Looking-Glass house

One thing was certain, that the WHITE kitten had had nothing to do with it:—it was the black kitten's fault entirely. For the white kitten had been having its face washed by the old cat for the last quarter of an hour (and bearing it pretty well, considering); so you see that it COULDN'T have had any hand in the mischief.

CHAPTER II. The Garden of Live Flowers

'I should see the garden far better,' said Alice to herself, 'if I could get to the top of that hill: and here's a path that leads straight to it—at least, no, it doesn't do that—' (after going a few yards along the path, and turning sharp corners), 'but I suppose it will at last. But how curiously it twists! It's more like a corkscrew than a path!

CHAPTER III. Looking-Glass Insects

Of course the first thing to do was to make a grand survey of the country she was going to travel through. 'It's something very like learning geography,' thought Alice, as she stood on tiptoe in hopes of being able to see a little further. 'Principal rivers—there ARE none. Principal mountains—I'm on the only one, but I don't think it's got any name. Principal towns—why, what ARE those creatures, making honey down there? They can't be bees—nobody ever saw bees a mile off, you know—' and for some time she stood silent, watching one of them that was bustling about among the flowers, poking its proboscis into them, 'just as if it was a regular bee,' thought Alice.

Types of Selectors continued

Class Selector

If you don't want all of your tags to appear exactly the same, you need a "free agent" selector that can be applied to any HTML tag. This is the *class selector*. When defining a class rule, you place a period immediately before the class name to let the browser know, "Hey, this is a class selector, not an HTML or ID selector":

.hilight { background-color: yellow;}

This says:

The hilight class text background color is yellow.

To apply this class (and thus its styles) to an HTML tag, add the class attribute to a tag with the class name in quotes. You can apply the same class to any HTML tag you choose, as many times as you want:

<h2 class="hilight">Chapter I...</h2>

Notice though that you do not add the period with the class name when it's in the HTML tag. The period is only included when you are setting up the class rule.

The hilight class text background color is yellow.

Class Selector

.hilight { background-color: yellow; }

Period

<h2 class="hilight"> Chapter I...</h2>

NO Periods

<p class="hilight"> 'I should...</p>

<h2 class="hilight">
Chapter I...</h2>

.hilight {color : red; }

<p class="hilight">
'I should...</p>

CHAPTER I. Looking-Glass house

One thing was certain, that the WHITE kitten had had nothing to do with it:—it was the black kitten's fault entirely. For the white kitten had been having its face washed by the old cat for the last quarter of an hour (and bearing it pretty well, considering); so you see that it COULDN'T have had any hand in the mischief.

CHAPTER II. The Garden of Live Flowers

'I should see the garden far better,' said Alice to herself, 'if I could get to the top of that hill: and here's a path that leads straight to it—at least, no, it doesn't do that—' (after going a few yards along the path, and turning sharp corners), 'but I suppose it will at last. But how curiously it twists! It's more like a corkscrew than a path!

CHAPTER III. Looking-Glass Insects

Of course the first thing to do was to make a grand survey of the country she was going to travel through. 'It's something very like learning geography,' thought Alice, as she stood on tiptoe in hopes of being able to see a little further. 'Principal rivers—there ARE none. Principal mountains—I'm on the only one, but I don't think it's got any name. Principal towns—why, what ARE those creatures, making honey down there? They can't be bees—nobody ever saw bees a mile off, you know—' and for some time she stood silent, watching one of them that was bustling about among the flowers, poking its proboscis into them, 'just as if

Types of Selectors continued

Class Selector: Dependent Class

A dependent class allows you to specify the styles a class should have if the class is applied to a particular HTML tag. This allows you to create a general style for a class, but then specify more styles for a specific HTML tag within that class. For example, you might set up a general class to make the background color yellow, and then set up a dependent class so that when that class is applied to a particular tag, the background color is green instead:

If the hilight class is used with a level 2 header, then its background color is green.

h2.hilight { background-color: green; }

If the hilight class is used with a level 2 header, then its background color is green.

Class Selector

h2.hilight { background-color: green; }

HTML Selector

<h2 class="hilight"> Chapter I...</h2>
<p class="hilight"> 'I should...</p>

h2.hilight { background-color : green; }

<h2 class="hilight">
Chapter I...</h2>

.hilight { background-color : yellow; }

<p class="hilight">
'I should...</p>

Through the Looking-Class | by Lewis Carroll

CHAPTER I. Looking-Glass house

One thing was certain, that the WHITE kitten had had nothing to do with it:—it was the black kitten's fault entirely. For the white kitten had been having its face washed by the old cat for the last quarter of an hour (and bearing it pretty well, considering); so you see that it COULDN'T have had any hand in the mischief.

CHAPTER II. The Garden of Live Flowers

'I should see the garden far better,' said Alice to herself, 'if I could get to the top of that hill: and here's a path that leads straight to it—at least, no, it doesn't do that—' (after going a few yards along the path, and turning sharp corners), 'but I suppose it will at last. But how curiously it twists! It's more like a corkscrew than a path!

CHAPTER III. Looking-Glass Insects

Of course the first thing to do was to make a grand survey of the country she was going to travel through. 'It's something very like learning geography,' thought Alice, as she stood on tiptoe in hopes of being able to see a little further. 'Principal rivers—there ARE none. Principal mountains—I'm on the only one, but I don't think it's got any name. Principal towns—why, what ARE those creatures, making honey down there? They can't be bees—nobody ever saw bees a mile off, you know—' and for some time she stood silent, watching one of them that was bustling about among the flowers, poking its proboscis into them, 'just as if
Done

Types of Selectors continued

Class Selector: Mix and Match Classes

As if being able to add a single class to an HTML tag wasn't enough, you can also add multiple classes to a single HTML tag, mixing and matching styles as needed. Simply list all of the classes you want applied to a particular HTML tag in the class attribute, separated by spaces:

<p class="hilight smallprint">'I should...</p>

When applied to an HTML tag, that tag picks up the styles of all of the classes applied to it.

Naming Your Classes and IDs

You can call your classes or IDs anything you want as long as you follow these basic rules:

- It can start with a letter or a number.

- It can contain any letter, number, hyphen ("-"), or underscore ("_").

- Both classes and IDs are case sensitive. So, "myClassName" is different from "myclassname".

Class or ID names could be "bob", "3423_jyt", or "9-8-2009", but you should always try to name them something meaningful according to what the class or ID is for, rather than what styles it applies. For example, I might call a class "redText" to hilight certain text. But what happens if later I want to make the hilighted text yellow? The yellow text is now created using a class called redText. A better choice would be to call the class something like "hilight" or "smallprint," which describes what it is for and allows for different versions.

The highlight class background color is yellow.
The smallprint class font size is extra small.

.hilight { background-color: yellow; }

.smallprint { font-size: x-small; }

<p class="hilight smallprint"> 'I should...</p>

Space

h2.hilight {color : yellow; }

<h2 class="hilight">
Chapter I...</h2>

.smallprint { font-size: x-small; }

<p class="hilight smallprint">
'I should...</p>

Through the Looking-Glass | by Lewis Carroll

CHAPTER I. Looking-Glass house

One thing was certain, that the WHITE kitten had had nothing to do with it:—it was the black kitten's fault entirely. For the white kitten had been having its face washed by the old cat for the last quarter of an hour (and bearing it pretty well, considering); so you see that it COULDN'T have had any hand in the mischief.

CHAPTER II. The Garden of Live Flowers

'I should see the garden far better,' said Alice to herself, 'if I could get to the top of that hill: and here's a path that leads straight to it—at least, no, it doesn't do that—' (after going a few yards along the path, and turning several sharp corners), 'but I suppose it will at last. But how curiously it twists! It's more like a corkscrew than a path!'

CHAPTER III. Looking-Glass Insects

Of course the first thing to do was to make a grand survey of the country she was going to travel through. 'It's something very like learning geography,' thought Alice, as she stood on tiptoe in hopes of being able to see a little further. 'Principal rivers —there ARE none. Principal mountains—I'm on the only one, but I don't think it's got any name. Principal towns—why, what ARE those creatures, making honey down there? They can't be bees—nobody ever saw bees a mile off, you know— and for some time she stood silent, watching one of them that was bustling about among the flowers, poking its proboscis into them, 'just as if it was a regular bee,' thought Alice.

Done

Types of Selectors continued

ID Selector

The first thing to know about the ID selector is that, on the surface at least, it looks and acts exactly like the class selector. The only obvious difference is that you use a hash mark at the beginning, to declare it, rather than a period:

#title01 { color: green; }

To apply the ID (and thus its styles) to an HTML tag, add the ID attribute to the tag with the name of the ID you want to apply:

<div id="title01">Chapter I...</div>

Similar to the class selector, you do not add the hash mark with the ID name when it's in the HTML tag. The hash mark is only included when you are setting up the ID rule.

What ID's Are Good For

So what's the difference between a class and an ID? It isn't so much in how these selectors work, but in what you use them for:

- Identifying major page sections (for example, header, content, footer)

- Identifying unique content or modules (for example, search, navigation, ad)

- Identifying an element to be used with Javascript

- Specificity, which we will talk about more in the next chapter

The title01 ID text color is green.

ID Selector

#title01 { color: green; }

Hash Mark

<h2 id="title01"> Chapter I... </h2>

NO Hash Mark

<h2 id="title01">
Chapter I...</h2>

#title01 { color : green; }

Through the Looking-Glass | by Lewis Carroll

CHAPTER I. Looking-Glass house

One thing was certain, that the WHITE kitten had had nothing to do with it:—it was the black kitten's fault entirely. For the white kitten had been having its face washed by the old cat for the last quarter of an hour (and bearing it pretty well, considering); so you see that it COULDN'T have had any hand in the mischief.

CHAPTER II. The Garden of Live Flowers

'I should see the garden far better,' said Alice to herself, 'if I could get to the top of that hill: and here's a path that leads straight to it—at least, no, it doesn't do that—' (after going a few yards along the path, and turning sharp corners), 'but I suppose it will at last. But how curiously it twists! It's more like a corkscrew than a path!

CHAPTER III. Looking-Glass Insects

Of course the first thing to do was to make a grand survey of the country she was going to travel through. 'It's something very like learning geography,' thought Alice, as she stood on tiptoe in hopes of being able to see a little further. 'Principal rivers—there ARE none. Principal mountains—I'm on the only one, but I don't think it's got any name. Principal towns—why, what ARE those creatures, making honey down there? They can't be bees—nobody ever saw bees a mile off, you know—' and for some time she stood silent, watching one of them that was bustling about among the flowers, poking its proboscis into them, 'just as if

Done

Styles in Context

When speaking, context can radically alter the meaning of a statement. Take the phrase:

"I'm going to kill you!"

If someone said that while whacking you on the head with a pillow, it would mean something very different than if they said it while whacking you on the head with a baseball bat. The context in which those words are spoken is the difference between the phrase being a playful euphemism or a menacing threat.

Likewise, in CSS, the context of a particular element can determine its style. For example, if you want headers in a sidebar to look different from headers in the main body, you can easily give each a different look by defining how the level 1 header tag should look in the body and a different rule for how it should look in a sidebar.

UGSMAG uses the *<h2>* tag in both their top article headline and in secondary headlines as well, using CSS to give the headlines a different size depending on which spot they appear in.

Styles in Context continued

Styles Based on Where Something Is

The most frequent way to use context is to style an element based on the HTML tags, classes, or IDs of its parent elements. Remember that an element is created anytime you put HTML tags around content. You can nest one element inside of another, and the surrounding tags are called parent elements. We can then write our CSS to style a tag based on the HTML tags, classes, or IDs that the element is within to style the *descendent selectors*.

A Simple Example of Descendent Selector Context

For example, you might style the text color *<cite>* tag—which is used to indicate that a block of text is a citation, such as a book title like *Through the Looking-Glass*—green, but make it red if it's in a level 1 header. To do this, we list each of the selectors that define the context, with a space in between:

A citation's text color is green.

cite { color: green; }

If a citation is in a level 1 header, its text color is red.

h1 cite { color: red; }

If a citation is in a level 1 header, its text color is red.

h1 cite { color: red; }

Space

<h1><cite>Through the Looking-Glass</cite></h1>

<h1><cite>
Through the Looking-Glass
</cite></h1>

h1 cite { color: red; }

Through the Looking-Glass | by Lewis Carroll

Quotes From *Through the Looking-Glass*

From Chapter 1 or *Through the Looking-Glass*.

'Oh, you wicked little thing!' cried Alice, catching up the kitten, and giving it a little kiss to make it understand that it was in disgrace. 'Really, Dinah ought to have taught you better manners! You OUGHT, Dinah, you know you ought!'

From Chapter 2 or *Through the Looking-Glass*.

'It's no use talking about it,' Alice said, looking up at the house and pretending it was arguing with her. 'I'm NOT going in again yet. I know I should have to get through the Looking-glass again—back into the old room—and there'd be an end of all my adventures!'

From Chapter 3 or *Through the Looking-Glass*.

'I think I'll go down the other way,' she said after a pause: 'and perhaps I may visit the elephants later on. Besides, I do so want to get into the Third Square!'

Done

Styles in Context <span>continued</span>

A More Complex Example of Descendent Selector Context

Context is not just for HTML tags. You can get as specific as you want about the context using classes and IDs as well. For example, we might create a rule for a *<cite>* tag if it's in the introduction of the article section of the page:

If a citation is in a paragraph with the intro class that is within the article ID, its text color is red.

#article p.intro cite { color: red; }

You can create contexts as specific as you like, but keep in mind it is always the last selector in the list that gets the actual styling.

The above CSS would apply its styles to the following content:

<div id="article"><p class="intro"><cite>
Through the Looking-Glass
</cite></p></div>

But not to:

<div id="article"><h1><cite>
Through the Looking-Glass
</cite></h1><div>

Because it doesn't have the *intro* class in a paragraph.

> *If a citation is in a paragraph with the intro class that is within the article ID, its text color is red.*

#article p.intro cite { color: red; }

Space

<div id="article"><p class="intro"><cite>
Through the Looking-Glass
</cite></p></div>

<div id="article"><h1><cite>
Through the Looking-Glass
</cite></h1></div>

<div id="article"><p class="intro"><cite>
Through the Looking-Glass
</cite></p></div>

#article p.intro cite { color: red; }

Through the Looking-Glass | by Lewis Carroll

Introduction to *Through the Looking-Glass*

As part of **Project Gutenberg**, the text for *Through the Looking Glass* was made available electronically to the Internet.

Directory

- Chapter I: Looking-Glass house
- Chapter II: The Garden of Live Flowers
- Chapter III: Looking-Glass Insects
- Chapter IV: Tweedledum and Tweedledee
- Chapter V: Wool and Water
- Chapter VI: Humpty Dumpty
- Chapter VII: The Lion and the Unicorn
- Chapter VIII: It's My Own Invention
- Chapter IX: Queen Alice
- Chapter X: Shaking
- Chapter XI: Waking
- Chapter XII: Which Dreamt It?

Done

Styles In Context   continued

Styles for Children

Styles can also discriminate between an element that is a direct child of its parent or an element that is a "grandchild," allowing you to style *child selectors*. For example, you can create a rule to make the text red only when it's the direct child (not a grand-child) of a paragraph tag.

If the emphasis tag is in a paragraph, and does not have any other parent tags, its color is red.

p>em { color: red; }

If we applied these two rules to the following HTML code:

<p><em>the white kitten</em><p>

Here, "the white kitten" will be red because the emphasis tag is a directly within the paragraph. However, if we applied it to this HTML code:

<p><strong><em>the old cat</em></strong></p>

In this case, "old cat" would not get the red styling because the strong text is the emphasized text's direct parent, not the paragraph.

IE6: Not Always in Context

Although IE7 and above rectifies the situation, IE6 does not support styling of child and sibling selectors. Make sure when using these contextual selector types that they are only used as a design enhance-ment or include a work-around for IE6 as described in Chapter 12, "The Last Word: Dealing with Browser Inconsistencies."

If the emphasis tag is in a paragraph, and does not have any other parent tags, its color is red.

$$p > em\{ color: red; \}$$

Chevron

$<p><em>$ the white kitten $</em></p>$

Through the Looking-Glass | by Lewis Carroll

Through the Looking-Glass

By Lewis Carroll

CHAPTER I. Looking-Glass house

$p>em\{ color : red; \}$

$<p><em>$
the white kitten
$</em></p>$

$<p><strong><em>$
the old cat
$</em></strong></p>$

One thing was certain, that *the white kitten* had had nothing to do with it:—it was the black kitten's fault entirely. For the white kitten had been having its face washed by ***the old cat*** for the last quarter of an hour (and bearing it pretty well, considering); so you see that it COULDN'T have had any hand in the mischief.

The way Dinah washed her children's faces was this: first she held the poor thing down by its ear with one paw, and then with the other paw she rubbed its face all over, the wrong way, beginning at the nose: and

Done

Styles In Context   continued

Styles for Siblings

If elements are next to each other (not nested inside of each other), they are called *adjacent* or *sibling selectors*. You can set a style based on an element's sibling. For example, let's say you want any citation that's next to emphasized text to be red:

If a citation is next to emphasized text, its text color is red.

em+cite { color: red; }

If we applied this to the following HTML:

<em>Quotes</em> from <cite>Through the Looking-Glass</cite>

The words "Thorough the Looking-Glass" would be red, because the *<em>* and *<cite>* tags are next to each other (despite the intervening text).

However, with the following HTML:

<em>Quotes</em> <strong>from</strong>
<cite>Through the Looking-Glass</cite>

The words "Through the Looking-Glass" would not get the red styling because the *<strong>* tag is in the way.

If a citation is directly next to emphasized text, its color is red.

$$em+cite\{\ color:\ red;\ \}$$

Plus Sign

<em> Quotes</em> from
<cite>Through the Looking-Glass</cite>

<em> Quotes/em> from
<cite>Through the Looking-Glass</cite>

em+cite{ color: red; }

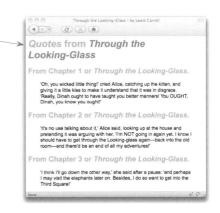

Styles for Special Cases

Although primarily intended to add styles to particular elements created using HTML tags, there are several cases where we can use CSS to style content on the page that is not specifically set off by HTML tags or to create a dynamic style in reaction to something that your Web site visitor is doing on the screen. These are known as pseudo-elements and pseudo-classes:

- **Link pseudo-classes**: Used to style hypertext links. Although primarily associated with color, you can actually use any CSS property to set off links and provide user feedback during interaction.

- **Dynamic pseudo-classes**: Used to style any element on the screen depending on how the user is interacting with it.

- **Pseudo-elements**: Used to style the first letter or first line in a block of text.

Link States

All hypertext links have four "states" that can be styled in reaction to a user action:

- a **link** state when there has been no action

- a **hover** state when the mouse cursor is over it

- an **active** state when the user clicks it

- a **visited** state when the user returns after having visited the linked-to page

Link

Hover

Active

Visited

Styles for Special Cases continued

Styles for Link Actions

Although the link tag can be styled just like any other HTML tag, it is a special case, because people visiting your site can interact with it. It's a good practice to create different styles to react to what the visitor is doing. To that end, CSS includes four different *pseudo-classes* for each of the four interaction states: *link*, *visited*, *hover*, and *active*:

The default link text color is red.

a:link { color: red; }

If the link is in the browser history, its text color is dark red.

a:visited { color: darkred; }

When the visitor hovers over a link, its text color is hot pink.

a:hover { color: hotpink; }

When the visitor clicks a link, its text color is fuchsia.

a:active { color: fuchsia; }

Collectively, these are known as the *link pseudo-classes*. They need to be in the above order—link, visited, hover, active—to function properly, due to the cascade order, which we'll learn more about in the next chapter. It's also important to remember that, while links are typically associated with color, any style can be applied to a link.

Designing Interaction

In Chapter 10, "Navigation" we'll double down on how to use the link and dynamic pseudo-classes to create a variety of interactive styles for buttons and other controls. It's important for you to expand your notion of Web site design to include the interactive elements. Often I see visual comps from designers that look great but are static. Don't ignore the fact that people are using your site.

The default link text color is
red.
If the link is in the browser history, its text color is
dark red.
When the visitor hovers over a link, its text color is
hot pink.
When the visitor clicks a link, its text color is
fuchsia.

a:link { color: red; }
a:visited { color: darkred; }
a:hover { color: hotpink; }
a:active { color: fuchsia; }

<a href="index.html">Welcome...</p>

Styles for Special Cases continued

Styles for Dynamic Actions

The hover and active states are not just for links. You can actually place your cursor over and click on any element on the screen and style elements for those actions. The third action state is when the user selects an element on the screen (usually a form field) and that element is in *focus* and it is ready for user input.

The default text color for the class formField in an input box is gray.

input.formField { color: gray; }

When the user hovers over an input field with the formField class, its text color is green.

input.formField:hover { color: green; }

When the user clicks an input field with the formField class, its text color is red.

input.formField:active { color: red; }

While the user is typing in an input field with the formField class, its text color is black.

input.formField:focus { color: black; }

Collectively these are called the *dynamic pseudo-classes*, which allow you to provide interactive feedback to the user. Dynamic pseudo-classes can be applied to any element on the screen but are chiefly used to add dynamic interaction to form fields and buttons, which we will look at in Chapter 10, "Navigation & UI"

One drawback: IE7 does not support active and focus, and IE6 supports none of these.

The default text color for the class formField in an input box is gray.
When the user hovers over an input field with the formField class, its text color is green.
When the user clicks an input field with the formField class, its text color is red.
While the user is typing in an input field with the formField class, its text color is black.

```
input.formField { color: gray; }
input.formField:hover { color: green; }
input.formField:active { color: red; }
input.formField:focus{ color: black; }

<input class="formField" type="text" />
```

Styles for Special Cases <span>continued</span>

Styles for Parts of a Paragraph

To draw attention to an introduction or opening statement, one common practice is to make the first letter or first line of text in a paragraph stand out from the rest of the text on the page. A paragraph is a block of text, so it has a first letter and a first line of characters, but they do not have specific HTML tags around them. To style these you can use *pseudo-elements* for the first-letter and first line:

The first letter of each paragraph is red.

p:first-letter { color: red; }

The first line of each paragraph is blue

p:first-line { color: blue }

Keep in mind, though, that this applies the style indiscriminately to all paragraph tags on the page. If we want to style only the first letter or line of the first paragraph in our content, we would need to style it based on its context as the first child of a particular element (let's ID it as *content*).

The first letter in a paragraph within any tag with the content ID has a color of red.

#content+p:first-letter { color: red; }

<div id="content"><p>One thing was certain...</p></div>

The only drawback to this method is that it will not work in IE6, which does not recognize the child context.

The first letter of each paragraph is red.
The first line of each paragraph is blue.

$$p\!:\!first\text{-}letter \; \{ \; color : red; \; \}$$

Colon

$$p\!:\!first\text{-}line \; \{ \; color : blue; \; \}$$

Colon

<p>One thing was certain...</p>

Through the Looking-Glass | by Lewis Carroll

Through the Looking-Glass

By Lewis Carroll

CHAPTER I. Looking-Glass house

<p>One thing was certain...</p>

One thing was certain, that **the white kitten** had had nothing to do with it:—it was the black kitten's fault entirely. For the white kitten had been having its face washed by **the old cat** for the last quarter of an hour (and bearing it pretty well, considering); so you see that it COULDN'T have had any hand in the mischief.

p:first-letter { color : red; }
p:first-line { color : blue; }

<p>The way Dinah...</p>

The way Dinah washed her children's faces was this: first she held the poor thing down by its ear with one paw, and then with the other paw she rubbed its face all over, the wrong way, beginning at the nose: and just now, as I said, she was hard at work on the white kitten, which was lying quite still and trying to

Done

threadless Tees
Nude No More

Guys ▾ Girls ▾ Participate ▾ Info ▾

🛒 **0** Items in your cart!
▶ CHECKOUT

ORDER STATUS | SERVICE & HELP

Full Catalog

Browse by size ↓

Browse by style ↓

Go to page: 1 2 3 4 ... 26 27   View all

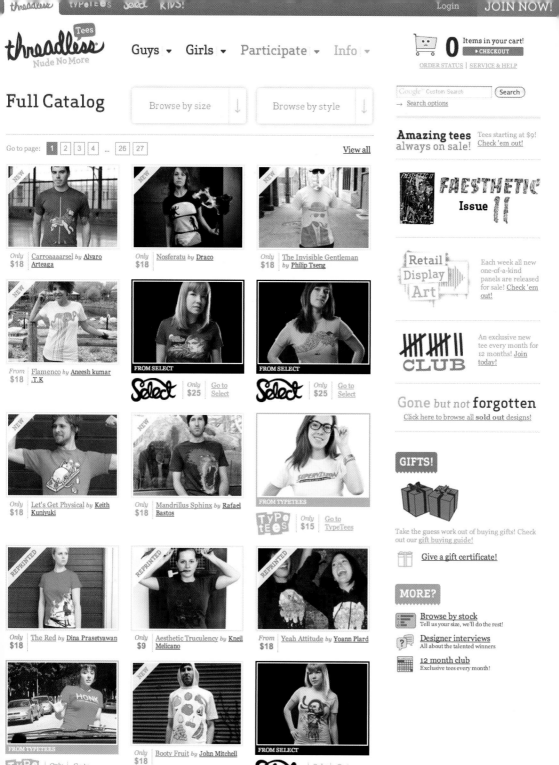

NEW
Only $18 | Carroaaaarsel by Alvaro Arteaga

NEW
Only $18 | Nosferatu by Draco

NEW
Only $18 | The Invisible Gentleman by Philip Tseng

NEW
From $18 | Flamenco by Aneesh kumar .T.K

FROM SELECT
Select Only $25 | Go to Select

FROM SELECT
Select Only $25 | Go to Select

NEW
Only $18 | Let's Get Physical by Keith Kuniyuki

NEW
Only $18 | Mandrillus Sphinx by Rafael Bastos

FROM TYPETEES
TypeTees Only $15 | Go to TypeTees

REPRINTED
Only $18 | The Red by Dina Prasetyawan

REPRINTED
Only $9 | Aesthetic Truculency by Kneil Melicano

REPRINTED
From $18 | Yeah Attitude by Yoann Plard

Only $18 | HONK

NEW
Only $18 | Booty Fruit by John Mitchell

FROM SELECT
Select Only $25 | Go to Select

FROM TYPETEES
TypeTees Only $15 | Go to TypeTees

NEW

NEW

NEW

Google Custom Search [Search]
→ Search options

Amazing tees always on sale! Tees starting at $9! Check 'em out!

FAESTHETIC Issue II

Retail Display Art — Each week all new one-of-a-kind panels are released for sale! Check 'em out!

CLUB — An exclusive new tee every month for 12 months! Join today!

Gone but not forgotten
Click here to browse all sold out designs!

GIFTS!
Take the guess work out of buying gifts! Check out our gift buying guide!

🎁 Give a gift certificate!

MORE?
Browse by stock — Tell us your size, we'll do the rest!
Designer interviews — All about the talented winners
12 month club — Exclusive tees every month!

When we speak to each other, we understand as much from the context of our words as from the words themselves. To be understood, we need to be clear about the context of our statements. We use semantics to do this, putting ideas together in a logical manner. We don't think about it, it's an instinct like breathing—we do it all the time.

In CSS, where you place your styles defines where and how they will be applied. You need to understand how styles cascade down the document, and how to apply different styles depending on the medium. With a bit of practice, the semantics of CSS will also become as instinctual as speaking or even breathing.

CHAPTER 5

SEMANTICS
MAKING SENSE OF STYLES

Where to Put Style Rules

In Chapter 4, I cleverly avoided showing you exactly where to put your CSS code. Instead I showed it disembodied from the HTML code it was intended to style. However, where you put your CSS code in relation to your HTML code has a direct impact on how it works and what elements it affects. There are three places to put your CSS code, depending on the scope of elements you want your styles to define:

01   **Inline** ↝ Styles placed directly into an HTML tag using the *style* attribute.

02   **Embedded** ↝ Styles placed in an HTML *<style>* tag and then applied to that Web page.

03   **External** ↝ Styles placed in a separate file and made accessible by any Web page using the *<link>* tag or *@import* rule.

Threadless

threadless.com

T-shirt styles in a well designed site—that's Threadless.

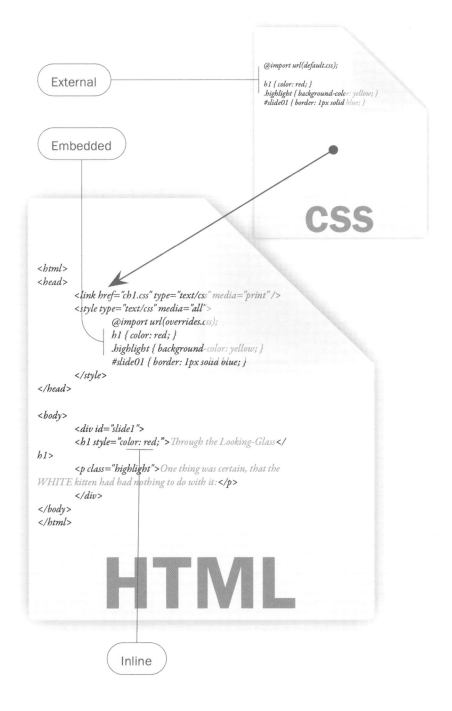

External

Embedded

```
@import url(default.css);

h1 { color: red; }
.highlight { background-color: yellow; }
#slide01 { border: 1px solid blue; }
```

CSS

```
<html>
<head>
        <link href="ch1.css" type="text/css" media="print" />
        <style type="text/css" media="all">
                @import url(overrides.css);
                h1 { color: red; }
                .highlight { background-color: yellow; }
                #slide01 { border: 1px solid blue; }
        </style>
</head>

<body>
        <div id="slide1">
        <h1 style="color: red;">Through the Looking-Glass</h1>

        <p class="highlight">One thing was certain, that the
WHITE kitten had had nothing to do with it:</p>
        </div>
</body>
</html>
```

HTML

Inline

Where to Put Style Rules continued

Inline Styles for an HTML Tag

So far, I have shown you examples of a complete CSS rule, consisting of a selector and a declaration:

h1 { color: red; }

However, CSS allows you to use the style attribute to place style declarations directly into an HTML tag:

<h1 style="color: red;">Through the Looking-Glass</h1>

This is called placing the style *inline*. It has the same effect on the style of the level 1 header tag as the full CSS rule, but only affects that single instance of the tag. All other level 1 headers on the page remain unaffected.

You can add as many different styles as you want to the style attribute, as long as you separate each declaration by a semicolon:

*<h1 style="color: red; font-family: Georgia; text-align: center;">
Through the Looking-Glass</h1>*

Although useful for quickly adding styles where they are needed in a design, inline styles have two major drawbacks that diminish the flexibility of CSS, so they should be used sparingly if at all:

01 Because inline styles affect only that one tag in that one
     instance, you can't easily make global changes to styles.

02 Inline styles are the final word on what styles are applied to
     that element, so they cannot be overridden.

I sometimes use inline styles while developing a site to quickly test out ideas, but before my Web pages go live, I take inline styles out of my HTML code and replace them with classes or IDs.

Style Attribute   Declaration

$<h1\ style="color:red;">$

Through the Looking-Glass

$</h1>$

HTML Tag

Inline Style:

Affects only the tag it is in.

Where to Put Style Rules continued

Embed Styles in a Web Page

Styles that are meant to affect an entire Web page (but not necessarily an entire Web site) are *embedded* into the HTML code using the HTML *<style>* tag, which will contain CSS rules:

<style type="text/css" media="all">

    h1 { color: red; }

    .hilight { background-color: yellow; }

    #slide01 { border: 1px solid blue; }

</style>

Embedded styles will be applied to any relevant elements in the page. Making a change to any of the rules in this list will affect all of the elements on the page that are affected by that rule. The type will always be "text/css" (yes, there are other types; no, no one uses them). We will discuss media types later in this chapter, but the default is "all," to tell the browser the styles should be applied to all media types.

Where to Place the Style Tag

You can place the *<style>* tag anywhere in the *<head>* or *<body>* of your HTML document, but I strongly recommended that you place this code in the *<head>* and above any JavaScript you might have on the page. Why? You want these styles to be applied as quickly as possible, before the content is displayed. If you place it after JavaScript or in the body of your HTML, there is a strong chance that the browser will start displaying the content before it has deciphered your style rules, and there will be an annoying flash as the page disappears and then reappears with the appropriate styling.

Style Tag   Style Type   Media Type

$$<style\ type="text/css"\ media="all">$$
$$h1\ \{\ color : red;\ \}$$
$$</style>$$

CSS Rule

Close Tag

Embedded Style:

Affects the entire page it is on.

Where to Put Style Rules continued

External Styles in a Web Site

Although inline and embedded styles allow you to add CSS to Web pages, the real power of CSS comes when you apply styles to an entire Web site. Instead of changes affecting a single page or tag, you can change dozens or thousands of pages by switching a single style. To do this, you need to set up an *external style sheet*, and then link it to a Web page or import it into a Web page or another external style sheet.

For example, say you have a Web page called *main.html*, with your content structured using HTML. To style this file, you would create an external style sheet called *default.css*, and place a *<link>* tag or *@import* rule in the HTML file pointing to the external style sheet. Those styles will now be applied to the Web page just as if the code was embedded in it. However, we could also link that same file to more files—for example *ch01.html* or *ch02.html*—and get the same styles applied to the content on those pages.

However, you are not limited to a single external style sheet. If you need to tailor the design of each page, you can link to or import additional style sheets to mix and match styles. For example, you can have a *ch01.css* and a *ch02.css* style sheet to customize those pages with their own backgrounds (or anything else you need). To cut down on the number of files you are linking to, you could import *default.css* into *ch01.css* and *ch02.css* to get the same results.

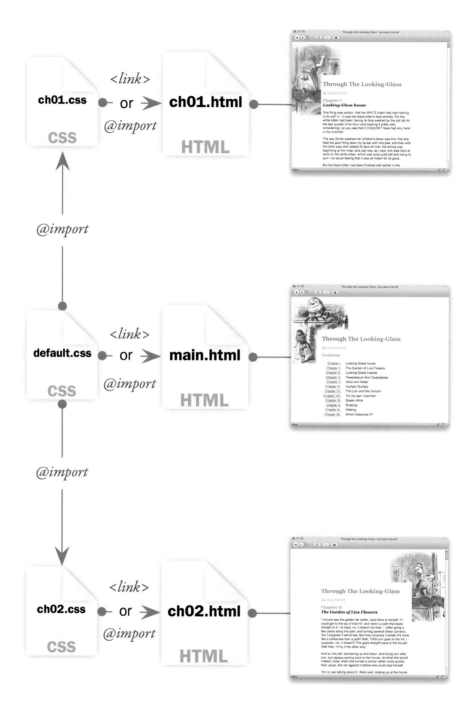

CSS

ch01.css

⊷ or ⟶

⟨link⟩

@import

ch01.html

HTML

Through The Looking-Glass

By Lewis Carroll

Chapter I
Looking-Glass house

@import

default.css

CSS

⊷ or ⟶

⟨link⟩

@import

main.html

HTML

Through The Looking-Glass

By Lewis Carroll

Contents

@import

ch02.css

CSS

⊷ or ⟶

⟨link⟩

@import

ch02.html

HTML

Through The Looking-Glass

By Lewis Carroll

Chapter II
The Garden of Live Flowers

Where to Put Style Rules continued

External Styles for a Web Site: Creating an External Style Sheet

Setting up an external CSS file is simple: Start a new file in your favorite text editor, and start typing in your CSS code. An external style sheet is simply a text file with your CSS code. That's it and nothing else. No HTML tags or JavaScript, just CSS. In fact, if you have anything else in the file other than CSS and notes (see the next section), the CSS will not work.

The code in the CSS text file might look like:

h1 { color: red; }

.hilight { background-color: yellow; }

#slide01 { border: 1px solid blue; }

Notice that there is no *<style>* tag around the CSS code.

When you are ready, save the file, giving it a meaningful filename with the extension *.css*. For example, You might have an external file called *default.css* and another one called *ch01.css*.

Since you may have multiple external style files for a single site, it's a good idea to collect them all into one place—usually a folder called *css*.

Which Text Editor is Best?

In Chapter 2, I recommended several different applications that you can use to edit your code. Any of those will work for creating an external style sheet. You could also use something simple like TextEdit (Mac) or NotePad (Windows). Avoid using a word-processor such as Microsoft Word, since it will add invisible characters that interfere with your code.

default.css

```
h1 { color: blue; }
h2 { font-size: 2em; }
.highlight { background-color: yellow; }
```

CSS

```
@import url(default.css);

h1 { color: red; }
.hilight01 { background-color: yellow; }
#slide01 { border: 1px solid blue; }
```

CSS

ch01.css

```
<html>
<head>
    <link href="ch1.css" type="text/css" media="print" />
    <style type="text/css" media="all">
        @import url(overrides.css);
        h1 { color: red; }
        .highlight { background-color: yellow; }
        #slide01 { border: 1px solid blue; }
    </style>
</head>

<body>
    <div id="slide1">
        <h1 style="color: red;"> Through the Looking-Glass</h1>
        <p class="highlight">One thing was certain, that the
WHITE kitten had had nothing to do with it:</p>
    </div>
</body>
</html>
```

HTML

Where to Put Style Rules continued

External Styles for a Web Site: Linking to an External Style Sheet

You have two options for adding external styles to your Web pages: linking or importing. The most common method is to use the *<link>* tag:

<link href="default.css" type="text/css" media="all" />

The *<link>* tag is a self-closing HTML tag that includes a reference to the external CSS file, which can either be a relative path (the location of the external file in relation to the HTML file that's pulling it in) or an absolute URL. As with the *<style>* tag, the *<link>* tag includes a type, which is always *"text/css"*, and a media type, which, for now, we'll set to *"all"* so that the styles are applied to any media type.

The *<link>* tag will inject the CSS code from the external style sheet wherever it is placed in an HTML document, just as if that code was embedded in the HTML file. As with embedding the code in the page, though, it's best to place the link within the *<head>* tag and above any JavaScript so that the styles are available as soon as the page is rendered in the browser window. Otherwise, you risk having the content load before the styles and then redraw itself after the styles have been processed.

You can add as many different link tags as you want to your Web page, allowing you to mix and match different styles. Before you go too crazy, though, study "The Cascade" section later in this chapter to understand how different CSS rules interact with and override each other.

Link Tag

< link
rel="stylesheet" — Link Relationship
href="default.css" — URL for File
type="text/css" — Style Type
media="all" — Media Type
/>

Self-Closing

Linked External Style:
Affects any page it is linked to.

Where to Put Style Rules continued

External Styles for a Web Site: Importing an External Style Sheet

The second way to add an external CSS file to your HTML code is using the *@import* rule, which can be added within any *<style>* tag you have embedded in a page, as long as they come before any other CSS code in the tag. You can also add them directly at the top of another external CSS file:

@import url(default.css);

Using the import rule will pull the CSS from the external file, placing it directly into that position in an HTML document or in another CSS file, based on the URL provided, either as a relative path (where the file is in relation to the summoning file) or an absolute path (the full URL, starting with *http://www*).

Like the *<link>* tag, you can add as many *@import* rules as you want to your external style sheets and HTML files, but it's important to understand how the cascade works (described later in this chapter) if you want your styles to work the way you intend them to.

Link or Import?

One important difference between *<link>* and *@import* is that the browser will wait for linked styles in the *<head>* to load before the page is displayed. *@import* allows the page to continue rendering and applies the styles afterwards. If your designs "blink"—with the content re-rendering to show the final design—this might be the reason why.

Import Rule

@import url(default.css);

URL for File

Imported External Style:

Affects any page or CSS file it is imported into.

Adding Notes to CSS

When creating designs, we often add notes and comments to remind us why we did something or to explain to people looking at the design after us what is going on. CSS allows us to add these notes, but they need to be set off from the rest of the text to ensure they don't interfere with the code. Open a CSS note with a slash followed by an asterisk. Then, reverse the pattern to close the note:

/ Note goes here */*

Anything you place between these two marks will be completely ignored by the browser, as if it did not exist. For example, you might want to add a one-line note about what a particular rule is doing:

/ Resets how content on the page is presented */*

Or you might want to add a multi-line note with details on who created the design and how they can be contacted for further details:

/————————————————*

By: Jason Cranford Teague

Email: jason@brighteyemedia.com

————————————————./*

Note that in this example, the extra dashes at the top and bottom are only there to help set off the comment from the rest of the page. They are not required.

Inheritance

It's important to remember that almost all HTML tags have styles indirectly applied to them. An inherited style can come from styles that are predefined by the browser itself (browser-default styles) or from an element's parent tags (parent-inherited styles).

For example, given the following style:

The hilight class's text color is purple.

.hilight { color: purple; }

And this block of HTML:

<h1 class="hilight">The Characters of
<cite>Through the Looking-Glass</cite></h1>

The book title, *Through the Looking-Glass,* will be purple because the citation tag inherits the style from the hilight class in its parent tag. However, it goes without saying that it will also be black, bold, and italicized because it is in the level 1 header, and italicized because of the citation tag. Now this may not come as any shock to you: Of course the *<h1>* tag makes text bold, but why? There is no mystical property of the universe that says when you invoke the alpha-numeric combination of "h1" that text will be bold. The text is bold because the person who created this browser decided to program it so that text in the header level 1 tag is bold. So, if no other styles override them, the text will at least have these default styles to make it stand out to anyone reading it.

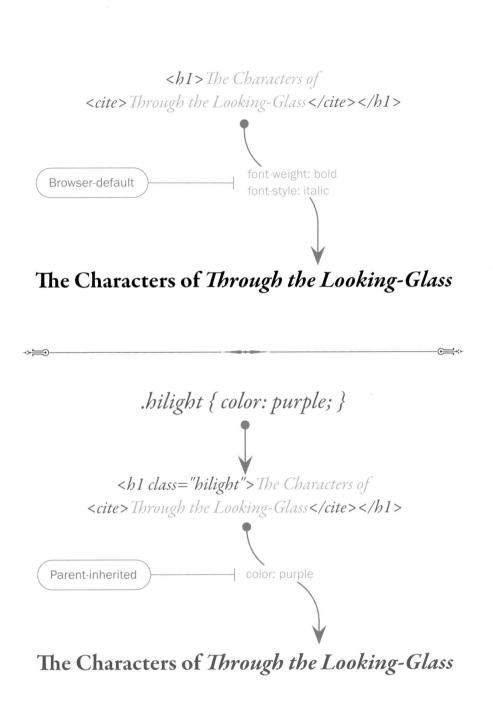

Inheritance continued

Overriding Inheritance

Style declarations are not engraved in stone and can be easily overridden. The most obvious way to override a style is to simply restate it later in your CSS. For example, if we wanted to override an inherited style, we might say something like:

The hilight class's text color is purple, but the cite tag's text color is orange.

cite { color: orange; }

.hilight { color: purple; }

In the following block of HTML:

<h1 class="hilight">The Characters of
<cite>Through the Looking-Glass</cite></h1>

the entire header will be purple because of the *hilight* class, but the book title, *Through the Looking-Glass,* will be recolored orange because the declaration for the citation tag overrides the parent-inherited style.

cite {color: orange; }

.hilight { color: purple; }

<h1 class="hilight">The Characters of

<cite>Through the Looking-Glass</cite></h1>

color: orange

The Characters of *Through the Looking-Glass*

Order

You can override a style for any selector simply by declaring the rule again with the same attribute but a different value:

.hilight { color: orange; }

.hilight { color: purple; }

The second instance of the *hilight* class will override the one before it, basically allowing you to change your mind.

The basic rule of thumb is that **the last instance of the style declared is the one applied to the page.**

Why would you want to override styles? This example shows the change immediately after, but that would not be very likely—you would just change the first rule. However, once your CSS starts getting longer and more complex, spanning multiple Web pages and multiple external CSS files, you may need to override the style set for one element on one page with another.

The order you place your CSS rules in will have a direct effect on which style ends up being applied, with the last one listed being the one that gets used, if there are no other overriding factors such as specificity, importance, and media type.

What are specificity, importance and media? Read on.

Overriding Inherited Styles

There are a lot of browser-default styles that are inherited by your Web pages. For example, we assume that text is black by default, or uses the Arial/Helvetica font family. Both of these are browser-default styles or are defaults controlled by the user that you can override using CSS.

.hilight { color: orange; }

.hilight {color: purple; }

<h1 class="hilight">The Characters of

<cite>Through the Looking-Glass</cite></h1>

color: purple

The Characters of *Through the Looking-Glass*

Specificity

Although the order you place your CSS rules in is important, it is not the final word in determining whether a style is applied to an element or not. *Specificity* refers to how much context you provide in a given CSS rule. The more specific the context the rule is to be applied, the more *weight* it is given when determining whether or not it is applied, even allowing you to override the order in which styles are set. If you are unsure what I mean by *context*, check Chapter 4's "Styles In Context" section first.

The basic rule of thumb is that **the more specific you are about the context of a CSS rule, the more likely it is that the style will be applied to the element.**

The more selectors included in your contextual rule, the more specific it is. If there are no other overriding factors—such as importance and media type—then a more specific rule gets applied regardless of order.

So, for example:

h1 .hilight { color: orange; }

is a more specific context than just:

.hilight { color: purple; }

The first CSS rule tells the browser how to style the *hilight* class if it is in a level 1 header tag, whereas the second rule only applies to the general case of the *hilight* class. And

#content h1 .hilight { color: brown; }

is even more specific, so it will win out over the other two rules that are placed after it in the style sheet.

h1 .hilight { color: orange; }

.hilight {color: purple; }

<h1>The Characters of
<cite class="hilight">Through the Looking-Glass</cite></h1>

color: orange

The Characters of *Through the Looking-Glass*

#content h1 .hilight { color: brown; }

h1 .hilight {color: orange; }

.hilight {color: purple; }

<h1>The Characters of
<cite class="hilight">Through the Looking-Glass</cite></h1>

color: brown

The Characters of *Through the Looking-Glass*

Specificity continued

Determining a CSS Rule's Weight

So what happens when you have the same number of selectors in a contextual rule that applies to the same element? For example:

#content h1 .hilight { color: purple; }

.column01 h1 .hilight { color: orange; }

Both of these CSS rules have three selectors, so which style is applied? In this case, you have to look at how many of each kind of selector appears in the rule. Each selector type—HTML, CSS, and ID—has its own specific weight when it comes to determining specificity. An HTML tag has a weight of 1, classes have a weight of 10, IDs have a weight of 100, and inline style (styles placed directly into an HTML tag with the *style* attribute) trump them all with a weight of ∞—that is, they cannot be overridden no matter how specific the CSS rule. In the example of above, the first CSS rule would have a weight of 111:

100 (#content) + 1 (h1) + 10 (.hilight) = 111

The second one has a weight of only 21:

10 (.column01) + 1 (h1) + 10 (.hilight) = 21

In this case, the first rule will be applied.

So, what happens in cases where the weights add up to be exactly the same? We fall back on order: The last CSS rule declared is the style used.

The basic rule of thumb is **any rule with ID selectors in the context is going to override most other rules; a rule with a class in the context will override a rule with just HTML selectors.**

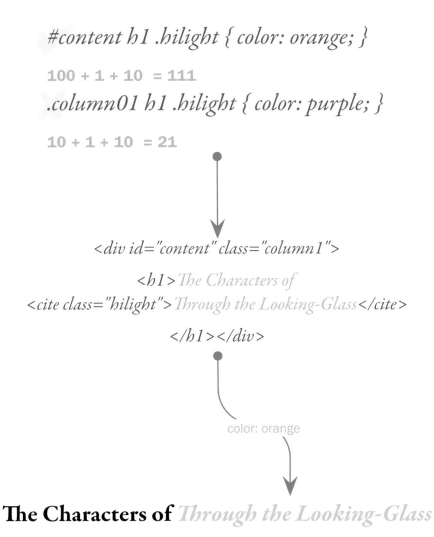

#content h1 .hilight { color: orange; }

100 + 1 + 10 = 111

.column01 h1 .hilight { color: purple; }

10 + 1 + 10 = 21

<div id="content" class="column1">

<h1> The Characters of
<cite class="hilight"> Through the Looking-Glass </cite>

</h1> </div>

color: orange

The Characters of *Through the Looking-Glass*

Importance

Inheritance, order, and specificity combine to determine which styles are applied to which elements, but you still have an ace in the hole if you need to force particular styles to be applied: *!important* will override all other concerns, forcing a style to be applied. By placing this immediately after a value—but before the semicolon—you are telling the browser that this is the most important style declaration being applied, overriding all other declarations, with the exception of inline styles.

For example, if you have rules for the same selector, but add *!important* to the first:

It's important that the hilight class text color is orange.

.hilight { color: orange !important; }

The hilight class text color is purple.

.hilight { color: purple; }

Despite the fact that the purple declaration is second, any text within the *hilight* class will be orange. *!important* will also override specificity:

#content h1 .hilight { color: orange; }

.column01 h1 .hilight {
  color: purple !important; }

Even though the first declaration to use orange for the text color has greater specificity, the second declaration will be used because it is important.

When Is a Style Important?

It could be tempting to throw *!important* on everything, which could come back to bite you later since they are hard to override. Important is best reserved for use while prototyping new ideas or if you are creating a module for another site where you need to override third-party styles.

.highlight { color: orange !important; }

.highlight {color: purple; }

<h1 class="hilight">The Characters of

<cite>Through the Looking-Glass</cite></h1>

color: orange

The Characters of *Through the Looking-Glass*

#content h1 .hilight { color: orange; }

.column01 h1 .hilight { color: purple !important; }

<div id="content" class="column1"><h1>The Characters of

<cite class="hilight">Through the Looking-Glass</cite>

</h1></div>

color: purple

The Characters of *Through the Looking-Glass*

Media

We generally think of the Web as a screen-based medium, but Web pages can be output on a variety of different devices. You need to be able to create style sheets that tailor your pages to a variety of media. Earlier in this chapter, when you learned how to add styles to a Web page or a Web site, I mentioned that you can also specify a *media type* to which the style sheet should be applied. The default is *all*—that is, **apply these styles regardless of the device**. Although CSS allows for several media types, really there are only four types you need to worry about:

01 ***Screen*** ∞ Whether it's a laptop or desktop computer; CRT, LCD, or plasma; *screen* is what you will use most of the time.

02 ***Print*** ∞ A lot of Web pages get printed. Some sites will create special "printer friendly" versions of the pages, but all you really need to do is add a printer style sheet. Whenever the user prints a page in a Web browser, this style sheet tailors the design for the printed page.

03 ***Handheld*** ∞ Handheld devices are a popular way to surf the Web, and you should provide a scaled-down version of your pages for that audience. Handheld devices present one of the greatest challenges, because of the variety of screen sizes.

04 ***All*** ∞ Styles will be used regardless of the device type.

For details on getting the best results with media types, check out Chapter 12: "The Last Word."

Screen

Print

Handheld

The Cascade

While the browser is rendering your Web page, each style declaration cascades through the Web page with a particular priority based on its media type, importance, specificity, order, and inheritance until its rule matches a particular element. (Sounds pretty poetic, doesn't it?) The cascade is predictable, and usually obvious as long as you don't try to overthink it.

Styles are applied in order of priority:

01 **Inline styles** ⟿ Inline styles trump all other priorities and are applied first.

02 **Media** ⟿ If the media type does not match the output media, then obviously the styles are ignored.

03 **Importance** ⟿ Any declaration with *!important* will be applied if there is not an overriding inline style.

04 **Specificity** ⟿ The more specific the context—weighted for the number of IDs, classes, and HTML selectors—the higher the priority for the style to be applied.

05 **Order** ⟿ The last style declared is the one that gets applied.

06 **Parent-inherited** ⟿ Any styles inherited from parent elements are applied.

07 **Browser-default** ⟿ Any styles inherited from the browser defaults are applied last.

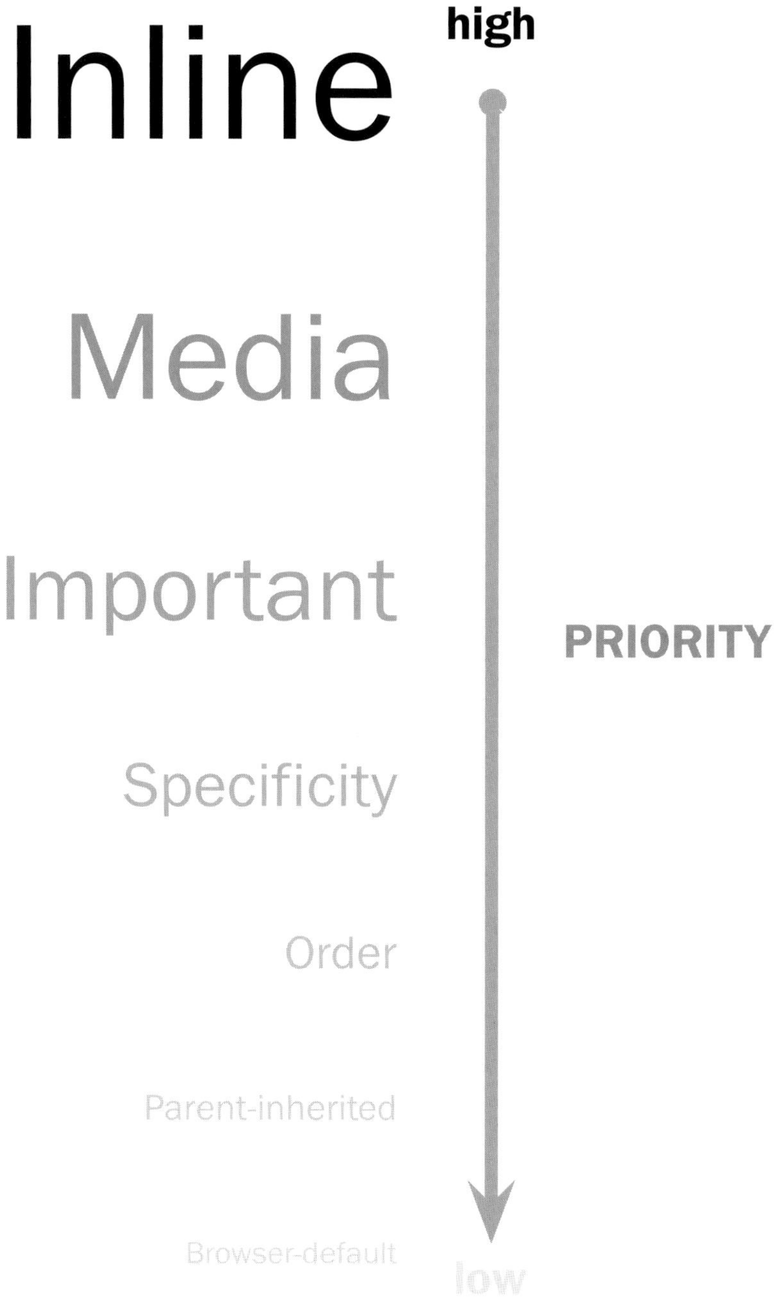

Inline _{high}

Media

Important

Specificity

Order

Parent-inherited

Browser-default

PRIORITY

Urban Dictionary is the slang dictionary **you wrote.** *Define your world*

3,990,777 DEFINITIONS WRITTEN SINCE 1999

Manufactured Outrage

MAY 24   838 up, 202 down

A falsified righteous outrage at things that are basically unimportant and meaningless, frequently employed by politicians, political activists, or the media. Politicians and talking heads use it to garner support for their causes, to claim the moral high ground and to tar their opponents; the media often just uses it in a cynical bid to increase ratings.

Manufactured outrages of note include `Nipplegate`*, the* `Monica Lewinski` *scandal, the 2009* `tea party`*s,* `backmask`*ed satanic lyrics,* `lapel pin` *controversies...*

Just about any time you hear any politician, activist, or radio show host getting outraged about anything, really. The louder and angrier they get, the harder they're working at manufacturing it.

by `Aquillion2` `share this` `more`

metatation

MAY 23   386 up, 1973 down

Metatation: The act of contemplating meditation itself, putting oneself outside the very state of meditation.

I was not satisfied with my meditation practice, so I began a metatation.

by `yubajeff` `share this` `more`

Self Qualified Referee

MAY 22   1696 up, 1482 down

Someone at any sporting event who always has to call the fouls, say the ref is wrong, or something similar even though nobody really listens to them and they don't have any idea what they are talking about. They think the ref is wrong about everything even though he gets paid to do it.

Soccer Mom-Oh, come on, that was such a foul!
Annoyed Observer-SHUT UP YOU SELF QUALIFIED REFEREE!!!

by `t12j19c95` `share this` `more`

missing link

MAY 21   2281 up, 1325 down

A man who is covered head to toe with thick and wiry hair. He's so hairy, he's the missing link that connects humans to apes.

Joe: "Damn, it's 115 degrees out here. Why doesn't Tom take off his shirt?"

Dick "That poor bastard is so hairy, he got tired of being called the missing link."

by `Crapholio` `share this`

Urban Dictionary hits your inbox with a **free new word** every day. We'll never spam you.

[you@example.com] [subscribe]

BIG UPS to **time magazine** for naming **urban dictionary** one of the 50 best websites of 2008

BUSTEDTEES

NEVER FORGET

NEW SHIRTS EVERY WEEK.

Urban Dictionary *gives you what's up on the street.*

ebizmark

NEW SUNDAY   676 defs   images   sounds

Blue Balls

e-depression

smarterchild

toronto maple leafs

elephant

peeps

Who does the *real* Bob

Vocabulary is what adds diversity to a language. In the examples I have presented so far, I kept the vocabulary simple so that we could concentrate on the syntax and semantics. Now, it is time to broaden your horizons—not to mention your design possibilities —with a slate of new CSS vocabulary.

I want to say up front that this is not a comprehensive list of CSS properties and values. It is a vocabulary list intended for designers to reference while working. But, just as when you are learning a new spoken language you wouldn't start off memorizing the dictionary, you don't need to know all of the nuances of the vocabulary to create great Web designs with CSS.

CHAPTER 6

VOCABULARY
TALKING THE TALK

Values

A CSS rule is made up of a selector with one or more declarations separated by semi-colons, and each declaration is made up of a property and a value (see Chapter 3 if you need more details). This chapter presents the various properties you will be using when describing your designs in CSS with a list of possible values underneath. The values come in two basic types: keywords and variables.

Keywords

Many of the values you will assign to a CSS property are keywords—words you type exactly as you see them—and most are self-explanatory, but a few need some additional explanation:

auto ✏← The browser calculates the value.

inherit ✏← Sets the property to use the same value as its parent element.

none ✏← Removes any specific value, which prevents the property from being displayed or removes any limitations.

normal ✏← Sets the property to its default value.

transparent ✏← Sets the color value to 0% opacity, allowing anything behind the object to show through. However, any length values associated with the property are still honored.

The Urban Dictionary

urbandictionary.com

If you need to know the meaning of a word

that you can't find in Webster's Dictionary, it's

probably in the Urban Dictionary.

Variables

Values listed in chevron brackets < > are variables. You will need to determine the exact value based on the type of variable:

See Appendix A for more details on values used in CSS.

<color> ☞ A chromatic value, based on the amount of red, green, or blue for the hue. Color values are most commonly expressed using the hexadecimal notation, RGB values (using percentages or the 0–255 scale), or as a keyword color name.

<font-name> ☞ The name of any font family you want to use. Keep in mind the browser can only use the font families that are installed on the end-user's computer.

See Appendix C for a list of Web-safe fonts.

<length> ☞ A relative or absolute length. Relative lengths vary based on context, while absolute values remain constant.

<number> ☞ An integer, either positive or negative.

<percentage> ☞ Generally calculated as a percentage of the inherited value. For example, if the parent's font size is 12px and the element's font size is 50%, then the rendered font will be 6px. Whenever a percentage value is required, what it is a percentage of will be indicated. For example: *<percentage-parents-font-size>*.

<url> ☞ A URL can either be a relative path or an absolute URL. If in doubt, use the absolute URL for a resource. Be careful, though, as this can cause trouble if you move the site to another location.

Fonts

Font properties apply directly to individual letter forms to change their nature and shape. These styles are generally associated with a unique version of the font within the same font family, or require that the computer create a *faux* version of the font on the fly. For example, italics are associated with a specific version of the font that has been created in the italic style—typically slanted and made to look more hand-written than the default style. However, if no such independent version of the font exists on the end user's computer, the browser will synthesize an italics version by slanting the default version by 15 degrees. Browser-synthesized fonts are not as readable or attractive as those created by a typographer, so it's best to use only styles with a true version of the font available.

font ⟷ The shorthand property that lets you set all of the font properties listed below at the same time, as well as line height. VALUES: *inherit* | *<font-style>* *<font-variant>* *<font-weight>* *<font-size>/<line-height>* *<font-family>*

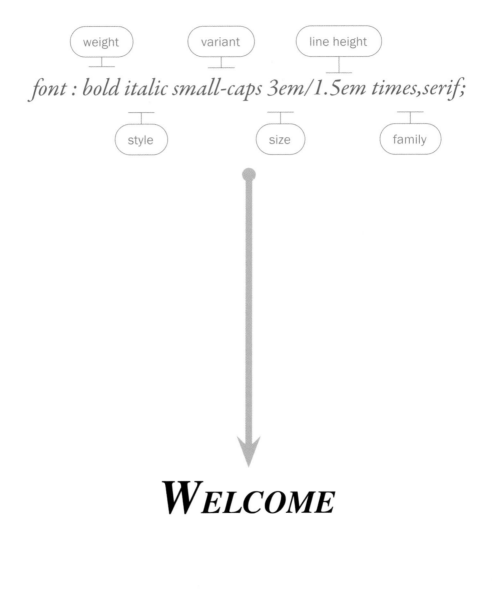

Fonts *continued*

font-family ⚬ Sets a specific font family by name or a generic font family of serif, sans-serif, monospace, handwritten, or fantasy. Font names with two or more words must be in quotes (for example, *"lucida sans"*). Generic values will use a font defined by the browser for that style.
VALUES: *inherit | <font-name> | serif | sans-serif | cursive | fantasy | monospace*
MULTIPLE VALUES: Include as many font-names as desired, separated by commas. The browser will try each font in sequence until it finds one it can use.

font-weight ⚬ The boldness of the font, generally a thicker version of the default. If a bold version of the font does not exist, the browser will simulate one based on the default pattern.
VALUES: *normal | bold | bolder | lighter | inherit*

font-variant ⚬ Sets the small-cap style, where all letters are capitals, but capitalized letters are slightly larger.
VALUES: *normal | small-caps | inherit*

font-style ⚬ Sets whether a font is italic or oblique. Most browsers will treat both values as italic if a true italic version of the font exists. If an italic version does not exist, the browser synthesizes an oblique version of the font by slanting the default version of the font to the right by 15 degrees.
VALUES: *normal | italic | oblique | inherit*

font-size ⚬ Sets an absolute-size, length, relative-size, or percentage based on the size of the font of the parent element.
VALUES: *<length> | <percentage-parents-font-size> | smaller | larger | xx-small | x-small | small | medium | large | x-large | xx-large | inherit*

font-family: garamond, georgia, serif;

Garamond, **Georgia**, Serif

font-weight: bold;

Bold

font-style: italic;

Italic oblique

font-variant: small-caps;

SMALL CAPS

font-size: 12px;

6px 12px 18px 24px

Text

Text styles are properties applied to an entire block of text within an element, but that do not affect the individual letters themselves. This includes text spacing properties such as letter, word, and line spacing, as well as text alignment, indents, underlining, overline, strike-through effects, and text capitalization.

color ❦ Sets the text color.
VALUES: *<color>* | *inherit*

letter-spacing ❦ Places an exact amount of space between each letter in a block of text to control the letter tracking. This is not to be confused with kerning , which uses data from the font to adjust spacing between letters based on pairing context. Letter spacing is a crude way to adjust spacing between letters, since it does not take into account the visual appearance of the letters. It is best reserved for large text such as headlines.
VALUES: *<length>* | *<percentage-font-size>%* | *inherit*

word-spacing ❦ Places an exact amount of space between each word in a block of text. Like letter spacing, this is a rough way to adjust spacing and is best used with large text.
VALUES: *normal* | *<length>* | *inherit*

line-height ❦ Controls the spacing between lines in a block of text. Adjusting line height to at least 1.5 (=150%) or higher is generally recommended to make large blocks of text more readable.
VALUES: *normal* | *<number>* | *<length>* | *<percentage-font-size>%* | *inherit*

white-space ❦ By default, Web browsers collapse multiple spaces in HTML code into a single space in the Web page and will automatically wrap text rather than allowing a horizontal scroll. White space allows you to override both of these defaults to preserve all white space or prevent text from wrapping.
VALUES: *normal* | *pre* | *nowrap* | *pre-wrap* | *pre-line* | *inherit*

color: rgb(128,0,0);

text is maroon

letter-spacing: .1em;

letters are spaced apart

word-spacing: 40px;

words   are   spaced   apart

line-height: 2;

One thing was certain, that
the white kitten had had
nothing to do with it: – it
was the black kitten's fault
entirely.

One thing was certain, that
the white kitten had had
nothing to do with it: – it
was the black kitten's fault
entirely.

One thing was certain, that
the white kitten had had
nothing to do with it: – it
was the black kitten's fault
entirely.

1   1.5   2

white-space: pre;

multiple   spaces   are   not collapsed

Text *continued*

text-align ⚬— Sets the justification of text to left, right, center, or full justification of the left and right edges.
VALUES: *left | center | right | justify | inherit*

vertical-align ⚬— Sets the vertical positioning of a block of text in relation to adjacent elements in the same line. Although seemingly useful for aligning elements, experience shows it does not behave as designers would expect, since it only works on inline elements and can not be used to vertically align blocks of text. The most common use is for super-scripting and sub-scripting text.
VALUES: *baseline | sub | super | top | text-top | middle | bottom | text-bottom | <percentage-line-height>% | <length> | inherit*

text-indent ⚬— Sets an indent for the first line in a block of text.
VALUES: *<length> | <percentage-width>% | inherit*

text-decoration ⚬— Sets a line to be placed over, under, or through the text in an element. The style of the line cannot be controlled and will be the same color as the text.
VALUES: *none | line-through | underline | overline | blink | inherit*

text-transform ⚬— Sets the capitalization of letters in a block of text, regardless of the state of the originating text.
VALUES: *lowercase | capitalize | uppercase | none | inherit*

text-align: center;

One thing was certain, that the white kitten had had nothing to do with it: – it was the black kitten's fault entirely.

One thing was certain, that the white kitten had had nothing to do with it: – it was the black kitten's fault entirely.

One thing was certain, that the white kitten had had nothing to do with it: – it was the black kitten's fault entirely.

One thing was certain, that the white kitten had had nothing to do with it: – it was the black kitten's fault entirely.

Left Center Right Justified

vertical-align: sub;

X^{super} X_{sub}

text-indent: 1em;

One thing was certain, that the white kitten had had nothing to do with it: – it was the black kitten's fault entirely.

text-decoration: strike-through;

~~One thing was certain, that the white kitten had had nothing to do with it: – it was the black kitten's fault entirely.~~

One thing was certain, that the white kitten had had nothing to do with it: – it was the black kitten's fault entirely.

One thing was certain, that the white kitten had had nothing to do with it: – it was the black kitten's fault entirely.

Line-through Underline Overline

text-transform: uppercase;

text case Text Case TEXT CASE

Lowercase Capitalize Uppercase

Background

All elements have a background that fills the area of its element box behind any content and padding, up to its border (see the next section for details on the element box). The background can be a solid color or an image that can be tiled, with its starting point positioned horizontally and vertically within the box.

background ⟿ The shorthand property that lets you set all of the background properties listed below at the same time.
VALUES: *<background-color> <background-image> <background-repeat> <background-attachment> <background-position> | none*

background-color ⟿ Sets the color to fill the area of an element behind the content up to its border. Any area of the background not covered by a background image will fill with the background color.
VALUES: *<color> | transparent | inherit*

background-image ⟿ Sets an image to appear behind the element's content and padding. You can use PNG (8, 24, or 32), JPEG, or GIF image formats.
VALUES: *url(<url>) | none*

background-attachment ⟿ Controls whether an image will scroll with the content of the element or stay fixed behind it.
VALUES: *scroll | fixed | inherit*

background: red url(bg-01.png) repeat scroll top 0;

color — image
repeat — attachment — position

background-color: rgb(126,0,68);

background-image: url(bg-01.png);

background-attachment: fixed;

Scroll   Fixed

Background *continued*

Image Repeat

For ideas on using backgrounds in layout, see Chapter 8, "Layout."

Background image tiling is how a lot of visual design is accomplished, so it's important to understand how the different tiling methods work and what they are for.

background-repeat ⬥ Controls whether or how the background image repeats (or not). You can set the background to tile, tile horizontally, tile vertically, or just appear once.
VALUES: *repeat | repeat-x | repeat-y | no-repeat | inherit*

repeat ⬥ Tiles the background image in the box horizontally and vertically to fill the entire area. Repeat is most often used for textured backgrounds.

no-repeat ⬥ The background image appears once and does not tile. Any area not covered by the background image is filled with the background color. No-repeat works well for watermarks and graphic bullets.

repeat-x ⬥ The background image tiles horizontally across the element. Any area below the tiling background is filled with the background color. Repeat-x is often used to create header designs by repeating a pattern or gradient across the top of an element.

repeat-y ⬥ The background image tiles vertically in the element. Any area of the box to the right of the tiling background is filled with the background color. Repeat-y is useful for creating column boundaries.

background-repeat: repeat;

background-repeat if position is set to 0,0

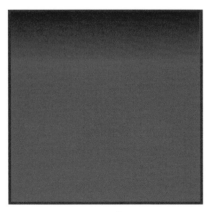

repeat

no-repeat

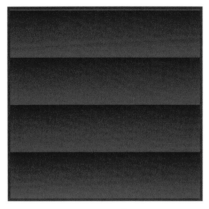

repeat-x

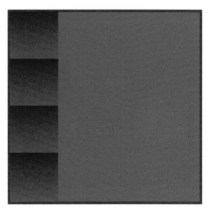

repeat-y

Background *continued*

Image Position

By default, all backgrounds are positioned in the top left corner of the element they are in, but you can offset that position in a number of different ways. Background positions can be set using one value or two values to set its horizontal and vertical positions.

background-position ☞ Uses one or two values separated by a space for the distance from the top or left side of the element to specify where the background will start to appear.
VALUES: *<length>* | *<percentage-box-width+padding>%* | *top* | *bottom* | *center* | *left* | *right* | *center* | *inherit*
MULTIPLE VALUES: **One** value for both top and left position, **two** values separated by a space for top and left respectively.

<length> ☞ Places the background a specified distance from either the top and/or left side of the element. For example, 0 0 is the top left corner. 10px 15px pushes the background starting point down 10px and over to the right by 15px.

<percentage-box-width+padding> ☞ Places the background a distance from the top and/or left side of the element, calculated as a percentage of the width or height of the element. For example, if the box was 10px by 20 px, and the background position is set to 25%, the background would be pushed down 5px and over to the right by 3px (rounding up from 2.5).

top ☞ Places the top of the background image against the top of the element.

bottom ☞ Places the bottom of the background image against the bottom of the element.

left ☞ Places the left side of the background image against the left side of the element.

right ☞ Places the right side of the background image against the right side of the element.

center ☞ Places the top and/or left corner of the background image in the center of the element.

background-position: 0 0;

position if background-repeat is set to repeat

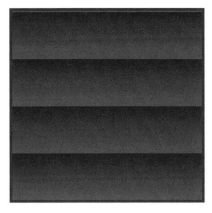

0 0

bottom 25px

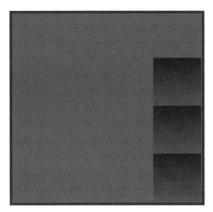

25px right

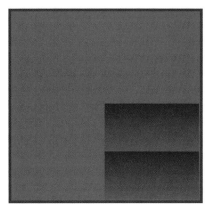

center center

Box

All elements are rectangular in shape—a box. Every time you add an HTML tag to create an element, you are creating an element box. All element boxes have a top, right, bottom, and left side that you can style, setting the margin, padding, border, width, and height, as well as the visibility and float.

Boxes can be set to automatically position themselves in context to surrounding boxes in one of two ways:

Inline boxes flow side-by-side horizontally, from left to right, with their left and right sides butting against each other, unless separated by a margin. Inline boxes will flow until they reach the right edge of the element and then will have a soft-return to the next line. Boxes that cannot break, such as images, will go off the right side and either be hidden or require a horizontal scroll.

Block boxes stack on top of each other vertically, with a hard return above and below the box, with bottom and top sides butting against each other, unless separated by a margin. Block boxes will continue down the page, requiring a vertical scroll if the height of the box does not allow all content to be shown.

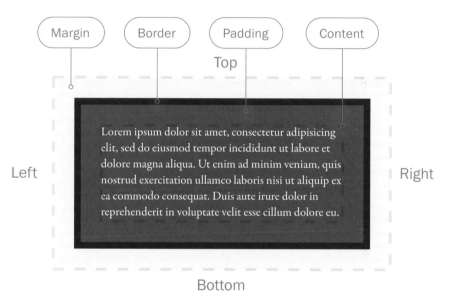

Element Box

Box *continued*

Display

All elements will have a default display type, which you can override using the display property that tells the element how to behave in relation to the elements around it.

display ⟜ Sets whether the element's box will be inline, block, a list item, or whether it appears at all. A value of none removes the element from the page completely so that a dynamic action can show it at the right time.
VALUES: *inline | block | list-item | none | inherit*

inline ⟜ Element boxes flow horizontally next to each other from left to right.

block ⟜ Element boxes flow vertically, stacking on top of each other from top to bottom.

list-item ⟜ Element boxes flow vertically, stacking on top of each other from top to bottom, like block, but with a list-marker and indented lines of text.

none ⟜ The element is completely removed from the document.

inherit ⟜ Uses the display style of the parent element.

Coming Soon: Inline-block

Although it's not ready for prime time yet (not even as a design enhancement) because it is not supported by IE6, another display type you may see in the future is *inline-block*, which allows you to insert a block element within an inline element. The effect is that the inline block element expands the line height of the line it is on to fit.

```
<span id="e1">Element 1</span>
<span id="e2">Element 2</span>
<span id="e3">Element 3</span>
```

#e1, #e2, #e3 { display: block; }

Block

#e1, #e2, #e3 { display: inline; }

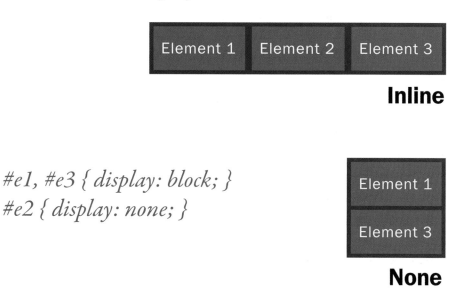

Inline

#e1, #e3 { display: block; }
#e2 { display: none; }

None

Box *continued*

Visibility

One way to hide an element is to set the display property to none and completely remove it from the document. If you want the element to remain in the document but be invisible, you have other options:

visibility Sets whether the box is visible or invisible. A hidden element will still take up space but will appear to be empty, like the invisible man in a rain storm.
VALUES: *visible* | *hidden* | *inherit*

opacity Sets the opacity of a box on a scale from 0.0 (clear) to 1.0 (opaque). This value affects the opacity of the element and all of its content and cannot be overridden by child elements. Opacity does not currently work in IE.
VALUES: *<0.0-1.0>* | *inherit*

filter: alpha(<0-100>) Sets the opacity of a box in IE on a scale from 0 (clear) to 100 (opaque). This is not a true CSS property, but it can be added to any CSS rule. If you set both the *filter: alpha* and the *opacity*, you can be sure you have the same value set for all browsers, including IE.

```
<span id="e1">Element 1</span>
<span id="e2">Element 2</span>
<span id="e3">Element 3</span>
```

#e1, #e3 { display: block; }
#e2 { visibility: hidden; }

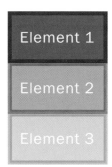

#e1 {   opacity: 1;
        filter: alpha(100); }
#e2 {   opacity: .5;
        filter: alpha(50); }
#e3 {   opacity: .25;
        filter: alpha(25); }

Box *continued*

Float

The float property has become crucial to multi-column Web layouts, as explained in Chapter 8, "Layout."

A floating element is one whose box aligns itself to the left or right. Surrounding content then wraps around it. This is often used to float images with or without captions, but can also be used for sidebars, pull quotes, or any other elements with a close association with the main text.

float ⟿ Positions the box to the left or right within its parent element. Any content below the element will wrap around it in moving up into the available space. If multiple elements are floated next to each other, then they will line up horizontally as space allows.
VALUES: *left | right | none | inherit*

clear ⟿ When applied to an element that has been placed below a floating element, floating stops, with the cleared element again appearing beneath the floating element. Floating can be specifically cleared on the left, right, or completely cleared on both sides.
VALUES: *none | left | right | both | inherit*

<p id="e1">Element 1</p>
<p id="e2">One thing was...</p>
<p id="e3">The way Dinah...</p>

#e1{

width: 75px;

height: 150px;

float: right; }

One thing was certain, that the white kitten had had nothing to do with it: -- it was the black kitten's fault entirely. For the white kitten had been having its face washed by the old cat for the last quarter of an hour (and bearing it pretty well, considering); so you see that it couldn't have had any hand in the mischief.

The way Dinah washed her children's faces was this: first she held the poor thing down by its ear with one paw, and...

Element 1

#e1{

width: 75px;

height: 150px;

float: right; }

#e3{ clear: right; }

One thing was certain, that the white kitten had had nothing to do with it: -- it was the black kitten's fault entirely. For the white kitten had been having its face washed by the old cat for the last quarter of an hour (and bearing it pretty well, considering); so you see that it couldn't have had any hand in the mischief.

Element 1

The way Dinah washed her children's faces was this: first she held the poor thing down by its ear with one paw, and...

Box *continued*

Width and Height

Width and height properties allow you to specify the dimensions of the content area of the box. Padding and border are then added to this to create the apparent width and height of the box, which is how much space it will take up in the design.

width ↝ Sets the horizontal length of the content area of the box.
  VALUES: *<length>* | *<percentage-parent-width>%* | *auto* | *inherit*

height ↝ Sets the vertical length of the content area of the box.
  VALUES: *<length>* | *<percentage-parent-height>* | *auto* | *inherit*

overflow ↝ Specifies how to treat excess content if the specified area for the box is not large enough to accommodate it. You can choose to hide the excess content, show the content, thus overriding the height value, force a scroll, or allow the browser to determine whether a scroll is needed or not (auto).
  VALUES: *hidden* | *visible* | *scroll* | *auto* | *inherit*

width: 225px;
height: 150px;
overflow: hidden;

Width = 225px

Height = 150px

One thing was certain, that the white kitten had had nothing to do with it: -- it was the black kitten's fault entirely. For the white kitten had been having its face washed by the old cat for the last quarter of an hour (and bearing it pretty well, considering); so you see that it couldn't have had any hand in the mischief.

The White Kitten

The way Dinah washed her children's faces was this: first she held the poor thing down by its ear with one paw, and then with the other paw she rubbed its face all over, the wrong way, beginning at the nose: and just now, as I said, she was hard at work on the white kitten, which was lying quite still and trying to purr -- no doubt feeling that it was all meant for its good.

Overflow

Box *continued*

Maximum and Minimum Width and Height

One of the key differences between designing for the Web and designing for other media, such as print or TV, is that the user controls the size of the browser viewport—the area in which your designs are viewed in—and can change the width and height at will. Instead of setting an absolute width and height, you also have the option of setting a width and height range to allow the content to stretch to fit the viewport area, while still not allowing it to shrink or grow to uncomfortable dimensions.

It is important to note that these properties do not work in IE6, so an absolute width and height should be set first to accommodate that browser.

max-width, max-height ↤ Sets the maximum width or height of an element. The element will grow to that size if the area is available, but no further.
VALUES: *<length>* | *<percentage-parent-width/height>* | *auto* | *inherit*

min-width, min-height ↤ Sets the minimum width or height of an element. The element will shrink to that size when the area is limited, but no further.
VALUES: *<length>* | *<percentage-parent-width/height>* | *auto* | *inherit*

max-width: 225px;
min-width: 150px;

max-height: 190px;
min-height: 150px;

├──────── Max-width = 225px ────────┤

One thing was certain, that the white kitten had had nothing to do with it: – it was the black kitten's fault entirely. For the white kitten had been having its face washed by the old cat for the last quarter of an hour (and bearing it pretty well, considering); so you see that it couldn't have had any hand in the mischief.

The White Kitten

Stretch

The way Dinah washed her children's faces was this: first, she held the poor thing down by its ear with one paw, and then with the other paw she rubbed its face all over, the wrong way, beginning at the nose: and just now, as I said, she was hard at work on the white kitten, which was lying quite still and trying to purr – no doubt feeling that it was all meant for its good.

Stretch

Max-height = 190px

Min-height = 150px

├──── Min-width = 150px ────┤

Box *continued*

Border

An element's border is the rule around its box on the top, right, bottom, and left. A border can have any thickness and color, and you can select from a limited number of styles. Set the border on all four sides to be the same, or set each side individually.

border ⟑ The *shorthand* property for setting all of the border properties for the box in one line, with values separated by a space. All three values must be declared in order for the border to appear.
Values: *<border-width> <border-color> <border-style>*

border-width ⟑ Sets the thickness of the border.
Values: *<length> | thin | medium | thick | inherit*
Multiple Values: **One** value for all four sides, **two** values separated by a space for top/bottom and left/right, or **four** values separated by spaces for top, right, bottom, and left, in that order.

border-color ⟑ Sets the hue of the border.
Values: *<color> | transparent | inherit*
Multiple Values: Same as *border-width*.

border-style ⟑ Sets one of the predefined border patterns.
Values: *none | dotted | dashed | solid | double | groove | ridge | inset | outset | inherit*
Multiple Values: Same as *border-width*.

border-top, border-right, border-bottom, border-left ⟑ The shorthand properties for setting the border properties on the indicated side of the box.
Values: *<border-width> <border-color> <border-style>*

border-width-top, border-width-right, border-width-bottom, border-width-left, border-style-top, border-style-right, border-style-bottom, border-style-left, border-color-top, border-color-right, border-color-bottom, border-color-left ⟑ Sets the indicated property for the indicated side of the box.
Values: Varies depending on property.

border: 5px solid rgb(67,0,37);

Top = 5px solid rgb(67,0,37)

Left = 5px solid rgb(67,0,37)

Right = 5px solid rgb(67,0,37)

One thing was certain, that the white kitten had had nothing to do with it: -- it was the black kitten's fault entirely. For the white kitten had been having its face washed by the old cat for the last quarter of an hour (and bearing it pretty well, considering); so you see that it couldn't have had any hand in the mischief.

The White Kitten

The way Dinah washed her children's faces was this: first she held the poor thing down by its ear with one paw, and then with the other paw she rubbed its face all over, the wrong way, beginning at the nose: and just now, as I said, she was hard at work on the white kitten, which was lying quite still and trying to purr -- no doubt feeling that it was all meant for its good.

Bottom = 5px solid rgb(67,0,37)

Box *continued*

Padding

Padding is the space between the content of the element's box and the border. Padding is easily confused with the margin, especially if there is no visible border. Padding, however, is intended to separate the content of the box from its edges, whereas the margin is meant to separate the element from other elements on the screen.

padding ☞ The shorthand property for setting the padding on all four sides of the box simultaneously.
VALUES: *<length>* | *<percentage-box-width>%* | *inherit*
MULTIPLE VALUES: **One** value for all four sides, **two** values separated by a space for top/bottom and left/right, or **four** values separated by spaces for top, right, bottom, and left, in that order.

padding-top ☞ Sets the space between the content and the top of the box.
VALUES: *<length>* | *<percentage-box-width>%* | *inherit*

padding-right ☞ Sets the space between the content and the right side of the box.
VALUES: *<length>* | *<percentage-box-width>%* | *inherit*

padding-bottom ☞ Sets the space between the content and the bottom of the box.
VALUES: *<length>* | *<percentage-box-width>%* | *inherit*

padding-left ☞ Sets the space between the content and the left side of the box.
VALUES: *<length>* | *<percentage-box-width>%* | *inherit*

padding: 35px 30px;

Top = 35px

One thing was certain, that the white kitten had had nothing to do with it: -- it was the black kitten's fault entirely. For the white kitten had been having its face washed by the old cat for the last quarter of an hour (and bearing it pretty well, considering); so you see that it couldn't have had any hand in the mischief.

The White Kitten

The way Dinah washed her children's faces was this: first she held the poor thing down by its ear with one paw, and then with the other paw she rubbed its face all over, the wrong way, beginning at the nose: and just now, as I said, she was hard at work on the white kitten, which was lying quite still and trying to purr -- no doubt feeling that it was all meant for its good.

Left = 30px

Right = 30px

Bottom = 35px

Box *continued*

Margin

The margin is the space between the border of an element and all other elements on the page. As mentioned, in the absence of a border or background, margin and padding will appear to be identical, but it is important to remember that they are different values. Margin should be used to adjust an element's position in relationship to other elements on the page, while padding should be used to keep content from bumping up against the edge of the box.

margin ⬥ The shorthand property setting the margin on all four sides of the box simultaneously.
VALUES: *<length>* | *<percentage-box-width>%* | *inherit*
MULTIPLE VALUES: **One** value for all four sides, **two** values separated by a space for top/bottom and left/right, or **four** values separated by spaces for top, right, bottom, and left in that order.

margin-top ⬥ Sets the space between the top of the box and the bottom of other elements.
VALUES: *<length>* | *<percentage-box-width>%* | *inherit*

margin-right ⬥ Sets the space between the right edge of the box and the left edge of other elements.
VALUES: *<length>* | *<percentage-box-width>%* | *inherit*

margin-bottom ⬥ Sets the space between the bottom of the box and the top of other elements.
VALUES: *<length>* | *<percentage-box-width>%* | *inherit*

margin-left ⬥ Sets the space between the left edge of the box and the right edge of other elements.
VALUES: *<length>* | *<percentage-box-width>%* | *inherit*

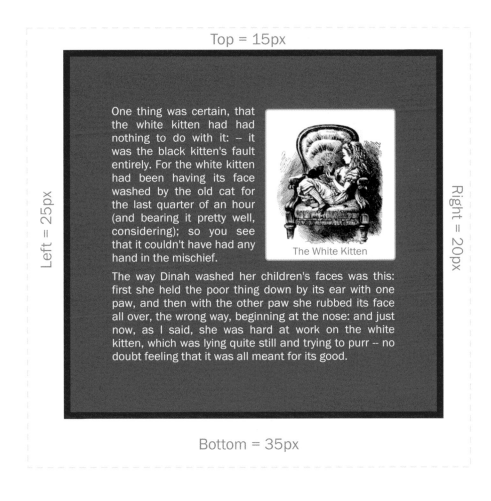

margin: 15px 20px 35px 25px;

Top = 15px

Left = 25px

Right = 20px

One thing was certain, that the white kitten had had nothing to do with it: – it was the black kitten's fault entirely. For the white kitten had been having its face washed by the old cat for the last quarter of an hour (and bearing it pretty well, considering); so you see that it couldn't have had any hand in the mischief.

The White Kitten

The way Dinah washed her children's faces was this: first she held the poor thing down by its ear with one paw, and then with the other paw she rubbed its face all over, the wrong way, beginning at the nose: and just now, as I said, she was hard at work on the white kitten, which was lying quite still and trying to purr -- no doubt feeling that it was all meant for its good.

Bottom = 35px

Box *continued*

Fixing IE

The CSS box model describes how an element should behave in your designs: The width and height are applied to the content area of the box, while padding and border lengths are added to get the *apparent width and height*, sometimes called the rendered width and height. At least, this is how the W3C CSS Work Group specified that the standard for the box model *should* work. Unfortunately, the folks who made IE6 didn't get the memo in time. They decided that width and height applied to the entire box, including the margin and padding.

You are OK as long as you do not set the width/height with padding and a border. But, as soon as you add padding and borders, in IE6 your designs will look different from standards-compliant browsers, even IE7.

Fortunately for us, the makers of IE6 missed another memo. When a declaration in a CSS rule has an underscore (_) in front of it, ignore the declaration. The upshot is that we can set a different width and/or height that only IE6 will see as long as we put an underscore at the beginning.

Known as the "underscore hack," this technique can be used anytime you need to provide a different value for IE6.

width: 225px;
padding: 10px;
border-width: 2px;

Width = 225px +
Left/Right Padding = 20px +
Left/Right Border = 4px
Apparent Width = 249px

⊢ Width = 225px ⊣

⊢ Width = 225px ⊣

⊢ Apparent = 249px ⊣

_width: 249px;

Underscore

⊢ Width = 225px ⊣

⊢ Width = 249px ⊣

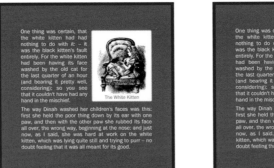

Position

All element boxes can be positioned on the screen, either relative to their natural position (where they would appear if left untouched) or absolute distance from the edge of its most immediate parent element with positioning set. To set the position of the box on the screen, you need to set both its position type and then its actual position.

Position Type

Think of setting the position type as turning on positioning. Until this is set, all elements have a "natural" position, which is where the element would appear if left untouched by positioning. To turn on positioning, you define how you want the element placed.

position ⊶ Defines the positioning type that the element's box will use.
   VALUES: *static | relative | absolute | fixed | inherit*

static ⊶ The element's box cannot be repositioned from its natural position.

relative ⊶ The element's box is positioned from where it would have natural position in the design.

absolute ⊶ The element's box is positioned relative to the immediate parent with a position type set.

fixed ⊶ The element's box is positioned relative to the browser window, and the element does not scroll with the rest of the page. Instead it stays fixed in its position.

inherit ⊶ The box inherits the position type from its most immediate parent with a position type set.

Fixed elements are a great way to create headers, footers, and menus that stay on the screen at all times. Unfortunately, *fixed* does not work in IE6. The good news is that you can use the box model (shown in Appendix C, "Fixing IE6") to set the position to absolute for that browser.

```
<span id="e1">1</span>
<span id="e2">2</span>
<span id="e3">3</span>
```

#e2{ position: relative; }

placement if top is set to 30px and left to 50px

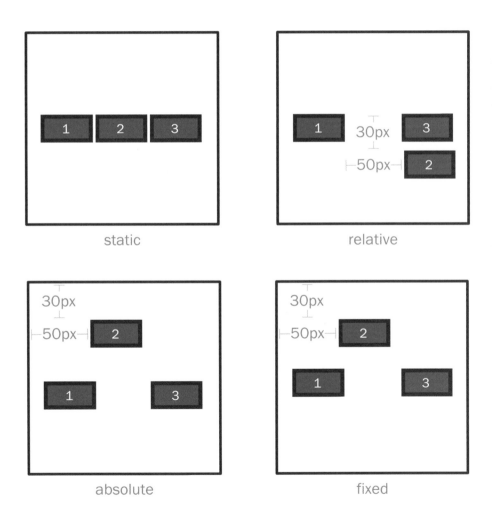

Position *continued*

Setting the 2-D Position

Setting the position type does not change an element's position. It merely prepares the element for one of the positioning properties to be applied to it.

top ⊶ Moves the element down from its normal position (relative) or from the top edge of its parent element (absolute), or top of the Web page (fixed).
VALUES: *auto* | *<length>* | *<percentage-parents-height>%* | *inherit*

right ⊶ Moves the element to the left from its normal position (relative) or from the right edge of its parent element (absolute), or right edge of the Web page (fixed).
VALUES: *auto* | *<length>* | *<percentage-parents-width>* % | *inherit*

bottom ⊶ Moves the element up from its normal position (relative) or from the bottom edge of its parent element (absolute), or bottom of the Web page (fixed).
VALUES: *auto* | *<length>* | *<percentage-parents-height>%* | *inherit*

left ⊶ Moves the element to the right from its normal position (relative) or from the left edge of its parent element (absolute), or left of the Web page (fixed).
VALUES: *auto* | *<length>* | *<percentage-parents-width>%* | *inherit*

<span id="e2">Element</span>

#e2{ top: 25px; }

placement if position is set to absolute

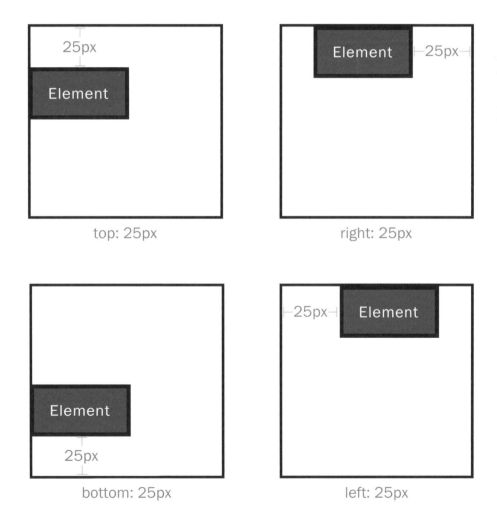

top: 25px

right: 25px

bottom: 25px

left: 25px

Position *continued*

Setting the 3-D Position

Once you start moving elements around, you may start stacking them in the Web page—one element appearing over top of or underneath another. By default the "natural" stacking order for elements (or z-index) is based on the order their code appears in the HTML. The first element has a z-index of 0 and its subsequent siblings increase their z-index by 1 (1, 2, 3, 4...) with higher numbers appearing above lower numbers. You can disrupt this natural order by changing the element's *z-index* property.

z-index ⬳ Sets the 3-D position of the box. Since positioned elements can overlap one another, z-index allows you to re-stack them as desired within their parent element by setting the level number to the level you want the element to appear. Higher numbers appear higher in the stack.
VALUES: *auto* | *<number>* | *inherit*

<span id="e1">1</span>
<span id="e2">2</span>
<span id="e3">3</span>

#e1{ z-index: 1; }

if positioned

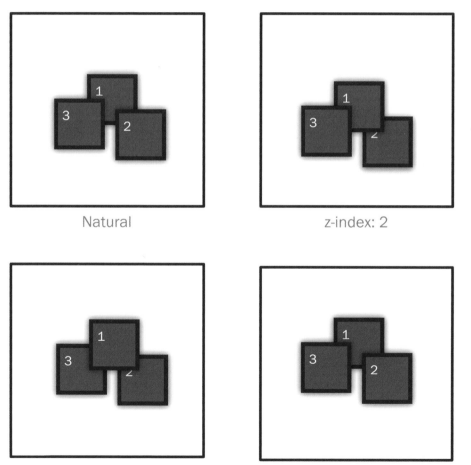

Natural

z-index: 2

z-index: 3

z-index: 0

Tables

Tables are used to present data. Any of the font, text, background, and box properties already mentioned can be applied to them. Tables have a few special styles, however, that can only be applied to the various table tags:

border-spacing: Sets the space between table data cells.
  Values: *<length>* | *inherit*
  Multiple Values: **One** value for all four sides, or **two** values separated by a space to set the top/bottom and left/right spacing separately.

border-collapse: Sets how borders between separate table data cells are treated. Use *collapse* to have borders between table data cells shared. Use *separate* to treat each table data cell as having independent borders.
  Values: *collapse* | *separate* | *inherit*

caption-side: Sets where a table caption appears, either above or below the table. Caption side does not work in IE6 or IE7, but will work in IE8, so you should consider this a design enhancement.
  Values: *top* | *bottom* | *inherit*

border-spacing: 6px 2px;

border-collapse: collapse;

collapse

separate

caption-side: top;

top

bottom

Lists

Lists are used for a variety of purposes in Web design, not the least of which is to actually create an ordered (*<ol>*) or unordered (*<ul>*) list of items. In addition, lists are often used to help organize links and menus, even if the actual list markers (bullets, letters, or numbers) are removed.

Although associated with particular HTML tags, any HTML tag can be used to create a list using these styles.

list-style ⸞ The shorthand property that lets you set all of the list properties listed below at the same time.
VALUES: *inherit* | *<list-style-type>* *<list-style-image>* *<list-style-position>*

list-style-type ⸞ Sets the marker style for the list.
VALUES: *disc* | *circle* | *square* | *decimal* | *decimal-leading-zero* | *upper-roman* | *lower-roman* | *upper-alpha* | *lower-alpha* | *lower-greek* | *none* | *inherit*

Learn about using CSS sprites in Chapter 10, "Navigation."

list-style-image ⸞ Sets an image file to be used as a marker. You can use PNG (8, 24, or 32), JPEG, or GIF image formats. This property is used much less than you might think. Most designers add graphic bullets to a list using the background-image property instead, using a technique called CSS sprites, which provides greater versatility.
VALUES: *url(<url>)* | *none* | *inherit*

list-style-position ⸞ Sets whether a list item's subsequent lines of text are indented (outside) or justified (inside).
VALUES: *inside* | *outside* | *inherit*

type

position

list-style: disc url(bullet-01.png)outside;

image

list-style-type: square;

- Disc
- Circle
- Square

A   Upper-Alpha
a   Lower-Roman
α   Lower-Greek

1   Decimal
01   Decimal-Leading-Zero
I   Upper-Roman
i   Lower-Roman

list-style-image: url(bullet-01.png);

list-style-position: inside;

Inside   Outside

Cursor

The dynamic pseudo-classes are explained in Chapter 4, "Syntax," in the section "Styles for Special Cases."

The mouse pointer provides visual feedback to the user when they interact with a given element. The cursor will automatically change for some elements such as links and form elements, but you can control how the cursor appears over any element using the dynamic pseudo-classes *:hover*, *:active*, and *:focus*.

cursor ⟾ Sets the appearance of a cursor. You can choose from the predefined list of cursors or specify a URL to load a PNG (8, 24, or 32), JPEG, or GIF image as your cursor.
VALUES: *default* | *url(<url>)* | *auto* | *crosshair* | *pointer* | *move* | *e-resize* | *ne-resize* | *nw-resize* | *n-resize* | *se-resize* | *sw-resize* | *s-resize* | *w-resize* | *text* | *wait* | *help* | *progress* | *inherit*

cursor: move;

default

+	crosshair	↑	n-resize
	pointer	→	e-resize
	move	↓	s-resize
	text	←	w-resize
	wait	↗	ne-resize
	help	↖	nw-resize
	progress	↘	se-resize
		↙	sw-resize

Exact icon appearance varies by browser and OS

171

Design Enhancements

There are a few properties on the cutting edge of CSS design that haven't been officially set as standards. While they may not be ready for prime time quite yet, because they may not be universally implemented, you can still use them to enhance your designs for those browsers that do use them.

Design enhancements should never be critical to your design or site functionality. Whether they work or not in a given browser should not prevent the visitor from using the site. The site just may not look quite as slick. In addition to the values, I'm listing which browsers each style works with. Keep in mind, though, that new versions are always coming out, so check out the *Speaking In Styles* Web site (*www.speaking-in-styles.com*) for up-to-date information.

Shadows

text-shadow ∞ Sets a drop shadow for text in an element. You can control the color, offset, and the amount of blur to get different shadow effects.
BROWSERS: Sa1.1
VALUES: *<color> <length-x-offset> <length-y-offset> <length-blur-radius>*

box-shadow, -moz-box-shadow, -webkit-box-shadow ∞ Sets a drop shadow for the box. You can control the color, offset, and the amount of blur to get different shadow effects. Although eventually the property will be called box-shadow, Firefox and Safari have implemented their own version: -moz and -webkit. Include all three to ensure cross-browser compatibility.
BROWSERS: Sa3, FF3
VALUES: *<color> <length-x-offset> <length-y-offset> <length-blur-radius>*

text-shadow: rgb(0,0,0) 4px 2px 6px;

Text Shadow

---

box-shadow: rgb(0,0,0) 4px 2px 6px;
-moz-box-shadow: rgb(0,0,0) 4px 2px 6px;
-webkit-box-shadow: rgb(0,0,0) 4px 2px 6px;

Design Enhancements *continued*

Rounded Corners

BROWSERS: Sa2, FF1.8

border-radius, *-moz-border-radius*, *-webkit-border-radius* ⚬⤙ Sets the roundness of box corners. Although eventually the property will be called simply border-radius, Firefox and Safari have implemented their own version: -moz and -webkit. For now, include all three to ensure cross-browser compatibility.
VALUES: *<length> | inherit*

Outline

BROWSERS: Sa2, FF1.8, Op9, IE7

The outline property creates a border around the box, similarly to the border property. Unlike a border, though, an outline cannot be controlled on a per-side basis and, most importantly, does not occupy any space. It will simply appear beneath any adjacent elements without disrupting the layout of the page.

outline ⚬⤙ The shorthand property that lets you set all of the outline attributes in one line, with values separated by a space.
VALUES: *<outline-width> <outline-color> <outline-style>*

outline-width ⚬⤙ Sets the thickness of the outline.
VALUES: *<length> | thin | medium | thick | inherit*

outline-color ⚬⤙ Sets the hue of the outline.
VALUES: *<color> | invert | inherit*

outline-style ⚬⤙ Sets one of the predefined outline patterns, which are the same as the border patterns.
VALUES: *none | dotted | dashed | solid | double | groove | ridge | inset | outset | inherit*

border-radius: 10px;
-moz-border-radius: 10px;
-webkit-border-radius: 10px;

outline: 10px solid rgb(67,0,37)

PART 3

In which the reader learns a tried and true process for Web development with CSS, how to create the many elements they will need in their designs, and reviews the best practices when speaking in styles.

SPEAKING LIKE A NATIVE

voxLIBRIS

Welcome

voxLIBRIS provides public domain audiobooks you can download free of charge.

GENRES

ABOUT

NEWS

REVIEWS

DONATE

CONTACT

Top 50 WTF Comic Moments
Countdown The Most Outrageous Moments In Comic Book History!
www.UGO.com/Comics

HP Global Citizenship
Why Protecting Privacy is Essential For Socially Responsible Companies
www.hp.com

Environments
Find Environments & More Environments Options Here!
Octopedia.com

Ads by Oogle

GENRES

Adventure
34 books

Anthropology
34 books

Children
34 books

Epic
34 books

Fantasy
34 books

History
34 books

Humor
34 books

Medical
34 books

Mystery
34 books

Philosophy
34 books

Romance
34 books

Science Fiction
34 books

About

Nulla sed felis. Sed et tellus. Vivamus venenatis suscipit magna. Vestibulum hendrerit iaculis nunc. Morbi posuere tempus elit. Ut commodo mattis nisi. **dictum ac, ante.** Vestibulum tortor.Vivamus elit. Nam nisi felis, egestas et, varius in, suscipit at, risus. Lorem ipsum dolor sit amet, consectetur adipiscing elit. Sed eget sapien.

Suspendisse aliquam suscipit elit. Sed a lorem. Suspendisse fermentum dolor in nibh dignissim bibendum. Etiam a eros et **dictum ac, ante** odio dapibus tempus. Phasellus ligula. Donec venenatis hendrerit tellus. Vestibulum dapibus augue at augue. Nulla imperdiet. Maecenas **dictum ac, ante** sed erat id neque lobortis elementum. Proin eleifend magna ac turpis. Curabitur magna sapien, convallis vitae, imperdiet non, sagittis aliquam, tellus. Nunc pretium orci cursus nisl facilisis pulvinar.

Read More

News

voxLIBRIS Adds 30 New Books

Lorem ipsum dolor sit amet, **consectetur adipiscing elit.** Vestibulum commodo metus sit amet libero. Cras nisl neque, lacinia id, mollis vel, **dictum ac, ante.** Vestibulum tortor.

Read More

New Categories Coming Next Month

Lorem ipsum dolor sit amet, consectetur adipiscing elit. Vestibulum commodo metus sit amet libero. Cras nisl neque, lacinia id, mollis vel, dictum ac, ante. Vestibulum tortor. **Lorem ipsum dolor sit amet.**

Read More

Reviews

Bowolf by Unknown

Lorem ipsum dolor sit amet, **consectetur adipiscing elit.** Vestibulum commodo metus sit amet libero. Cras nisl neque, lacinia id, mollis vel, **dictum ac, ante.** Vestibulum tortor.

Read More

Dead Men's Money by J.S. Fletcher

Lorem ipsum dolor sit amet, consectetur adipiscing elit. Vestibulum commodo metus sit amet libero. Cras nisl neque, lacinia id, mollis vel, dictum ac, ante. Vestibulum tortor. **Lorem ipsum dolor sit amet.**

Read More

TOP BOOKS

Through the Looking Glass
by Lewis Carol

Princess of Mars
by Edgar Rice Burroughs

Through the Looking Glass
by Aesop

Gods of Mars
by Edgar Rice Burroughs

My guess is that you already have your own personal or professional Web design process in place. Whether you are into Agile, UML, waterfall, or something of your own devising, I'm not here to upset the apple cart—maybe just add a couple of extra apples to it. If you are a designer, CSS needs to become a central part of your Web design process.

Using CSS is likely to change how you approach Web design. Although you may still create wire frames and comps, you'll find yourself making refinements, adjustments, and wholesale changes in CSS code. You may even find yourself going straight from hand-drawn sketches to CSS code. You'll save time and effort, and, before you know it your Web designs will start to really pop.

CHAPTER 7

DESIGNING WITH CSS

The Process: An Overview

Once upon a time, it was enough for the designer to create a few visual comps, maybe cut the chrome, and then hand everything over to a developer. If you followed this process you probably found that the developer never got things exactly the way you wanted them: Elements didn't line up, fonts were wrong, colors shifted. Never send a developer to do a designer's job. It doesn't matter how great your comps look in Photoshop; what matters is what the visitor sees in the Web browser. To get things right, it's important to become familiar with every aspect of the process, and be able to step in to guide the final outcome.

01 **Plan your site.** Before you code, think carefully about what you are doing, why you are doing it, and how you are doing it: sketching, wire-framing, mood boards, and visual comps are the best ways to plan before creating your site with CSS.

02 **Build your site.** One of the most important differences between print and Web design is not paper versus screen, but static versus dynamic. The great advantage of Web design is that you can make changes at anytime, and with CSS, you can make those changes extremely quickly. Prototypes allow you to test ideas in context.

03 **Deploy your site.** Take your prototype online to test it in the wild before finally going live with the hard launch.

voxLibris

speaking-in-styles.com/book/voxlibris

I'll be using the fictitious site voxLibris in the next several chapters to show the design process. All of the code used to create this page is listed in Appendix A.

04 **Iterate the process.** Creating a Web site is an iterative process. You can't just love it and leave it. Never be afraid to go back to anywhere within the process and make changes based on feedback.

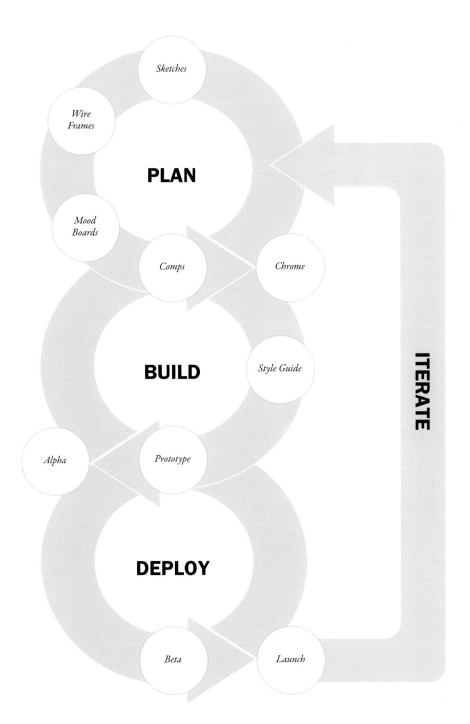

Plan

Every project should start with a plan. Whether it's in your head or formally spelled out, you need to define what the expectations are for the project's success. As the designer, your job is to conceive the successful design solution using a process of discovery and iteration. As you create your plans in advance of actual coding, it's important to keep in mind how you will actually realize your vision in code.

Sketches

Sketches are not meant to be detailed or complete plans, but to help you get the rough ideas down and capture notes about the project and rough dimensions. I like to put information like the Web site's purpose, audience, and content, as well as the site's message in big letters to remind me what this project is about. In addition, I'll quickly throw down different page types, mark stuff out, redraw them as necessary to experiment, looking for different design angles.

There are a lot of different ways to sketch. I carry my Moleskin graph paper sketchbook everywhere I go, ready to whip out when inspiration strikes (or when I have a few spare minutes). If I'm brainstorming with a group, I'll get pasteboard-size paper and start sketching while others throw out ideas. I've even been known to do digital sketches in programs like Microsoft Visio and OmniGraffle, which can then quickly evolve into wire frames.

The most important thing to remember about your sketches is to keep them fluid. Try as many different design solutions as you can come up with—never be tied to any one solution.

VOX LIBRIS

PAGES — Template
- MAIN
- ~~Book Cover~~ Browse
- ~~Book Text~~

Content
- Cover Images
- Book Info
- Book Text
- about VL

PURPOSE
- Download free audio books
- Download free book texts
- Learn about VL
- Donate to VC

WHO
- Audio book-ophiles
- Researchers
- Readers

MESSAGE — "It's About the Books!"

Book covers!, N

980px

VOX LIBRIS   100px

WELCOME   Favorites
            Index

200px

MAIN

VOX LIBRIS   Search

Reader

BROWSE

VL:48

Book

50k VOX LIBRIS
    Small header?

Plan *continued*

Page Flow

The first question you need to ask yourself when starting your design is "Will my page be fluid or fixed?" Although fluidity is generally considered for the width of the design, it can equally be applied to the height of the design. While most Web designs are based on a fixed width with a fluid height (that is, it stretches to the height required to display all of the page content), this is not your only option:

- **Fixed width/fluid height**: The page width is constrained, generally to prevent horizontal scrolling, and the height will stretch to accommodate the content, requiring a vertical scroll if it doesn't fit in the browser window.

- **Fluid width/fluid height**: The page stretches horizontally and vertically to use the maximum area available in the browser window. Content that does not fit in the area of the open browser window will require a vertical scroll to view.

- **Fixed width/fixed height**: Both width and height are constrained. How content that does not fit is treated will depend on how the overflow attribute for the box is set. Generally, with this design, content is carefully controlled so as not to require more space than the available area, or scrolling is controlled on a per module basis.

- **Fluid width/fixed height**: The page stretches horizontally to fill the available area and can even cause the page to scroll horizontally.

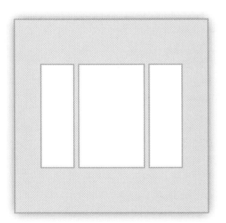

Fixed Width/Fluid Height

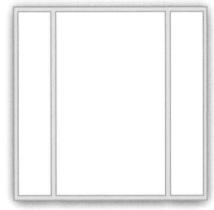

Fluid Width/Fluid Height

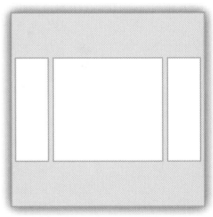

Fixed Width/Fixed Height

Fluid Width/Fixed Height

Plan *continued*

Wire Frames

Wire frames are your chance to plan the structure of your page without the distractions of visual design. They serve as the blueprints for construction and need to include placement and measurements of elements in pixels. Here are the basic elements you will need to include:

- **Fluid or fixed**: Determine whether the layout is fluid or fixed. Fluid layouts allow visitors to make better use of their screen real estate, but are generally harder to design to. For general fixed page widths, I use 980px, which will allow most visitors to see everything.

- **Widths**: Widths should be exactly specified in fixed layouts, but can be exact or variable—generally indicated with an asterisk (*)—in fluid designs.

- **Heights**: Heights should generally be variable, unless you know the element needs a fixed height. In those cases, make sure to account for how overflow content will be treated.

- **Margins**: Margins and padding should be indicated, but may need to be adjusted in the visual comps.

- **Scroll lines**: Although not as important as it used to be, the "fold" of the page should be indicated for different monitor resolution heights so that you know roughly where the page "fold line" will fall. I use heights of 290px , 410px, and 578px.

- **Color**: Use color only to indicate controls and links. Generally, I use blue to show actionable items and grayscale for everything else.

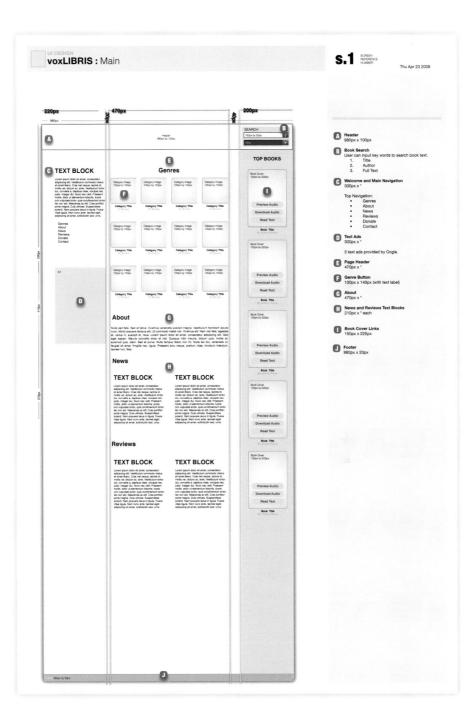

A Header
980px x 100px

B Book Search
User can input key words to search book text.
1. Title
2. Author
3. Full Text

C Welcome and Main Navigation
300px x *

Top Navigation:
- Genres
- About
- News
- Reviews
- Donate
- Contact

D Text Ads
300px x *

3 text ads provided by Oogle.

E Page Header
470px x *

F Genre Button
100px x 140px (with text label)

G About
470px x *

H News and Reviews Text Blocks
210px x * each

I Book Cover Links
150px x 225px

J Footer
980px x 20px

Plan *continued*

Mood Boards

There are many kinds of mood boards—everything from collages of seemingly random elements that reflect the desired style to boards that are on the verge of being a design specification document. The style you choose should depend on your own strengths as well as the needs of your client. If you are a strong visual designer, a poster style format may work best; if you are an information architect, a more structured document might be appropriate. Whatever style you choose, think carefully about what will best communicate the flavor of the site you want to create.

Mood boards are meant to help define the visual style of your site without you actually designing the entire interface. Generally, you can quickly create two or three "looks" that can then be presented to a client for feedback, without having to get bogged down in the details of building the pages. You can include splashes from the color palette, patterns, textures, typography, photos, and illustrations. I also recommend including treatments of some of the standard user interface elements such as form fields, lists, and tables.

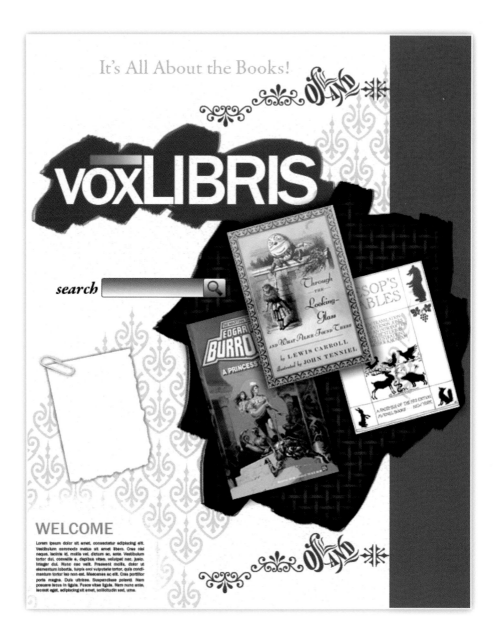

It's All About the Books!

voxLIBRIS

search

WELCOME

Lorem ipsum dolor sit amet, consectetur adipiscing elit. Vestibulum commodo metus sit amet libero. Cras nisl neque, lacinia id, mollis vel, dictum ac, ante. Vestibulum tortor dui, convallis a, dapibus vitae, volutpat nec, justo. Integer dui. Nunc nec velit. Praesent mollis, dolor ut elementum lobortis, turpis orci vulputate tortor, quis condimentum tortor leo non est. Maecenas ac elit. Cras porttitor porta magna. Duis ultrices. Suspendisse potenti. Nam posuere lacus in ligula. Fusce vitae ligula. Nam nunc ante, laoreet eget, adipiscing sit amet, sollicitudin sed, urna.

Plan *continued*

Visual Comps

Visual comps (short for compositions) combine the wire frames to create mood boards: a static version of what the final Web page will look like. If you skipped the mood boards, you may also be relying on the visual comps to present to your client, possibly showing several different skins for them to choose from. If you are working with a developer who will be constructing the site, this needs to be a pixel-perfect composition.

Once you get more comfortable with creating Web pages in CSS, however, you may find that you can be less thorough, and can leave some of the final design polishing until the prototype stage. Here are some tips to keep in mind for your visual comps:

- Use guides to reconstruct the grid you created in your wire frames as precisely as possible. You may ultimately want to break out of that grid to a less blocky design, but you need to know where the grid is to break it.

- Think carefully about how a background element will tile. You can tile horizontally or vertically to fill an area with a pattern. Complex background patterns that don't tile are possible but generally lead to larger graphic file sizes.

- If you want to use rounded corners or drop shadows, consider creating these with CSS as design enhancements. They are hard to create graphically but are easily added using CSS. Keep in mind that these styles are not currently supported in all browsers.

- If using Photoshop, make sure your proof setup (*View>Proof Setup*) is set to RGB; otherwise your colors will look very different in the browser.

Build

The faster you can move from planning to building, the better. It's easy to get bogged down trying to plan for every contingency, to the point that the planning takes over the production. Planning should give you direction, but, in an iterative design process, you can always revisit wire frames and comps as the situation on the ground changes.

Cutting Chrome

Putting the chrome back together to create your interface is covered in detail in Chapter 11, "Chrome."

Chrome (any graphics or visual effects used to create the user interface of a Web site) is generally cut from the visual comps. How you cut the chrome depends on the software you use to create your comps, but regardless of your software of choice, there are a few guidelines to follow while you are working:

- Most chrome is added as a background image using CSS, rather than as an image tag.

- Use transparent PNGs where possible to make overlapping elements easier to create. In Photoshop, this means using PNG 24. ImageReady allows you to create transparent PNGs in both PNG 8 and PNG 36, although not in PNG 24 for some reason.

- Use JPEGs for complex images such as photos.

- Combine different states of a chrome graphic into a single file, and use CSS sprites to slide it back and forth.

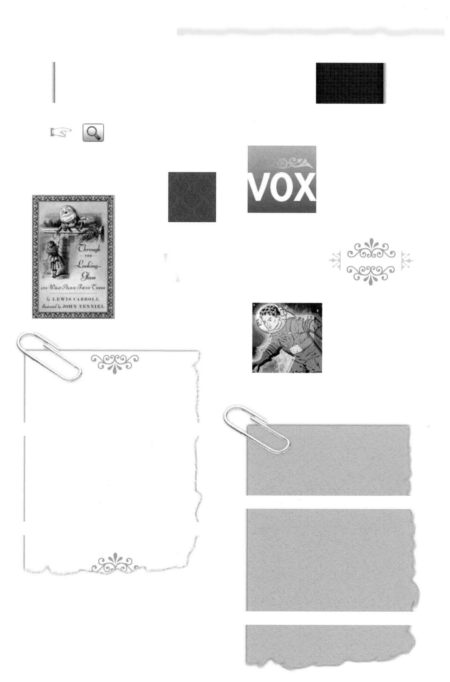

Build *continued*

The Style Guide

The style guide pulls all of your planning together into a single document, which is then a common point of reference for everyone on the team when building the site. It serves as a blueprint for constructing the site and provides notes for designers and developers who may work on the site in the future.

You should include the following information in your documents, using CSS style notation:

Typography is covered in Chapter 9, "Typography."

Typography: The font families, styles, and weights being used. You do not need to specify exact sizes or usage here. That will be included in the default styles. Because this is Web design, though, you want to include a prioritized list of fonts, starting with the most desired and ending with a generic font-family as the ultimate fallback option.

Color values are detailed in Appendix B, "CSS Values."

Colors: List all of the primary and secondary colors used in the site, giving the hex and RGB values for each. I also like to give each color a specific project name, which generally makes it easier to reference during discussions and feedback.

Default styles and layout are covered in Chapter 8, "Layout."

Default styles: Defines the global styles such as font-family, font-size, color, and page background that will be used over most of the pages.

Layout: The widths, height, padding, and margins of every element in the Web page.

Chrome is covered in Chapter 11, "Chrome."

Chrome: For each element, show the image(s) with file name(s) being used to create it.

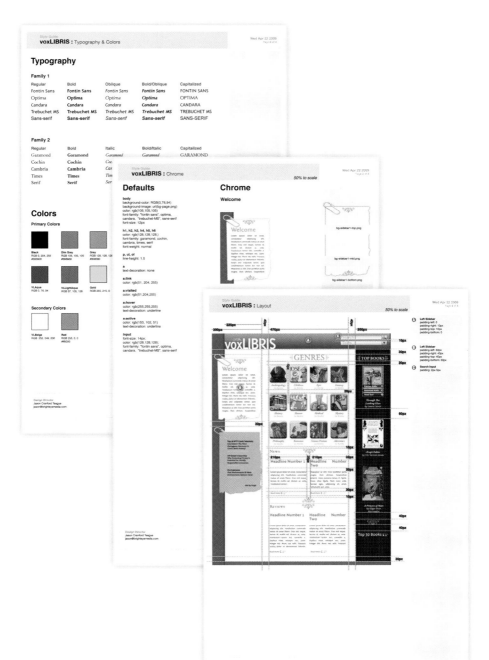

Page 1 (voxLIBRIS: Typography & Colors)

Typography

Family 1

Regular	Bold	Oblique	Bold/Oblique	Capitalized
Fontin Sans	**Fontin Sans**	*Fontin Sans*	***Fontin Sans***	FONTIN SANS
Optima	**Optima**	*Optima*	***Optima***	OPTIMA
Candara	**Candara**	*Candara*	***Candara***	CANDARA
Trebuchet MS	**Trebuchet MS**	*Trebuchet MS*	***Trebuchet MS***	TREBUCHET MS
Sans-serif	**Sans-serif**	*Sans-serif*	***Sans-serif***	SANS-SERIF

Family 2

Regular	Bold	Italic	Bold/Italic	Capitalized
Garamond	**Garamond**	*Garamond*	*Garamond*	GARAMOND
Cochin	**Cochin**	*Coc*		
Cambria	**Cambria**	*Car*		
Times	**Times**	*Tim*		
Serif	**Serif**	*Ser*		

Colors

Primary Colors

Black	Dim Gray	Gray
RGB 0, 204, 255	RGB 105, 105, 105	RGB 128, 128, 128
#000000	#696969	#808080

VLAqua	VLLightAqua	Gold
RGB 0, 78, 94	RGB 37, 105, 128	RGB 255, 215, 0

Secondary Colors

VLBeige	Red
RGB 252, 249, 230	RGB 255, 0, 0
	#ff0000

Design Director
Jason Cranford Teague
jason@brighteyemedia.com

Page 2 (voxLIBRIS: Chrome)

Defaults

body
background-color: RGB(0,78,94)
background-image: url(bg-page.png)
color: rgb(105,105,105)
font-family: "fontin sans", optima,
candara, "trebuchet-MS", sans-serif
font-size: 12px

h1, h2, h3, h4, h5, h6
color: rgb(128,128,128,)
font-family: garamond, cochin,
cambria, times, serif
font-weight: normal

p, ul, ol
line-height: 1.5

a
text-decoration: none

a:link
color: rgb(51, 204, 255)

a:visited
color: rgb(51,204,255)

a:hover
color: rgb(255,255,255)
text-decoration: underline

a:active
color: rgb(153, 102, 51)
text-decoration: underline

input
font-size: 14px;
font-family: "fontin sans", optima,
candara, "trebuchet-MS", sans-serif

Chrome

Welcome

bg-sidebar1-top.png

bg-sidebar1-mid.png

bg-sidebar1-bottom.png

Design Director
Jason Cranford Teague
jason@brighteyemedia.com

Page 3 (voxLIBRIS: Layout)

Left Sidebar
padding-left: 0
padding-right: 10px
padding-top: 10px
padding-bottom: 0

Left Sidebar
padding-left: 30px
padding-right: 40px
padding-top: 40px
padding-bottom: 30px

Search Input
padding: 3px 5px

Design Director
Jason Cranford Teague
jason@brighteyemedia.com

Build *continued*

Prototype

Ready to start coding? The prototype is where you transform your static visuals into living Web pages. If you are starting a prototype from scratch (rather than re-skinning an existing site), you will want to create your HTML first to define the general page structure to which the CSS is then applied. Keep these tips in mind while coding your CSS:

- **Don't be afraid to modify your design as you assemble it.** This is the difference between theory (the visual comp) and practice (the prototype). Often what works in the free-form world of the comp doesn't work in the more structured world of CSS code. For example, I used a different flourish with the "Genres" title than shown in the comp, because it proved impossible to code effectively. Remember: iterate.

- **Use placeholder content.** The closer you can get to the final content you will be using, the better, but don't waste time trying to get the exact content you will use for launch. For example, greek text for copy is fine at this point, as long as it is approximately the same length as the final copy.

- **Show an example of all use cases.** Try to replicate a sample of every element that will be on the page to show how it works. For example, add dummy links to show how they will be presented.

- **Test, test, test!** As you develop your prototype, make sure to constantly test it in as many browsers as possible. Nothing is more frustrating than finding your design looks great in Firefox but falls apart in Internet Explorer.

If you need to generate greek text (also known as "Lorem Ipsum" text) for your placeholder content, use the Web site *lipsum.com*.

Build *continued*

Prototype: Writing Your CSS

How you organize the various rules in your style sheet can affect your workflow and how quickly you can make changes. Of course, you can always just throw your styles together haphazardly, but when your style sheets get longer and longer, you will find yourself spending more and more time tracking down rules to make changes. Keep these tips in mind:

- **Cascade**: Remember that styles cascade, so once a style is set for a parent element, it is set for all of its children. For example, setting the *font-family* property in the *body* HTML selector means that font family is applied to all text on the page.

- **Versatility**: Any styles you create without having to resort to adding an image will significantly increase the design's versatility, making it easier to make adjustments and re-design later.

- **Easy to edit**: As your CSS code gets longer and more complex, it can get harder to find and edit code. Even if it takes a little more time, anything you can do to make it easier to sort through it all will save you time and frustration in the long run.

- **File size**: Every letter, number, space, and character adds to file size. They may seem like grains of sand, but get enough sand and you fill a beach. The larger the file size, the longer it takes to download. That's not to say that you have to agonize over every space you type, but try to cut code by using the cascade wherever you can.

Once you are ready to deploy your site, consider reducing your CSS file size by stripping out all of the comments and unnecessary spaces using a service like csscompressor.com.

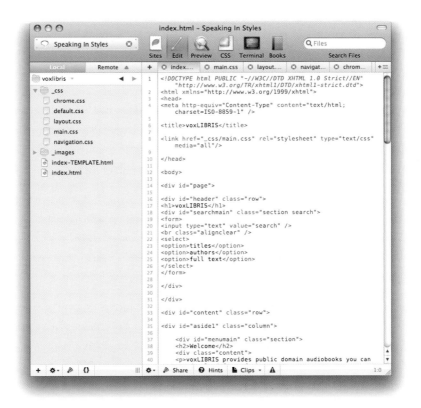

Build *continued*

Prototype: Organizing Your CSS

Here are a few tips on formatting and organizing your styles to make them easier to edit:

For a full listing of the code used to create the voxLibris template, see Appendix A.

- **Place general styles at the top of the style sheet** (01–46). This sets the default styles for your Web page—most importantly for the *<body>* element, which is the parent to all other elements. Remember, once a style is set in a parent tag, you never need to set it again unless you want to override it for a specific element. Since the body tag is the ultimate parent for all tags, anything you set there will be applied to all tags on the page, with the exception of form elements.

- **One declaration, one line** (example: 28). If you have only a single declaration for a rule, run it on a single line.

- **Use shorthand properties** (example: 11). Many styles have a shorthand property that collects one or more styles into a single line of code. These save time and space and are easier to find and edit in long lists of code.

- **Indent your declaration.** Use spaces and returns to make reading the code easier.

- **Organize rules by use** (example: 15–17). Group your rules together based on the elements they affect in the Web page, separating each group with notes. This lets you quickly track down a style based on its location on the Web page.

- **Organize by context** (example: 89). Within a grouping, group rules with similar contexts. Generally, if two rules have similar contexts, they will be closer to each other on the page, so if you see one, it makes it easier to find the other.

```css
01   /*--------------------------------------------------------
02          Reset Browser Inherited Styles
03   ----------------------------------------------------*/
04   html, body, div, span, applet, object, iframe, h1, h2,
          h3, h4, h5, h6, p, blockquote, pre, a, abbr,
          acronym, address, big, cite, code, del, dfn, em,
          font, img, ins, kbd, q, s, samp, small, strike,
          strong, sub, sup, tt, var, dd, dl, dt, li, ol, ul,
          fieldset, form, label, legend, table, caption,
          tbody, tfoot, thead, tr, th, td
05   {
06          margin: 0;
07          padding: 0;
08          border: 0;
09          outline: 0;
10          background: none;
11          font: inherit inherit 100% inherit;
12          text-align: left;
13          vertical-align: baseline;
14          list-style: none;      }
15   /*--------------------------------------------------------
16          Default Styles
17   --------------------------------------------------------
                  -*/
18   body, input, select {
19          color: rgb(105,105,105);
20          font-family: "fontin sans", optima, candara,
                  "trebuchet-MS", sans-serif;      }
21
22   h1, h2, h3, h4, h5, h6 {
23          color: rgb(128,128,128);
24          font-family: garamond, cochin, cambria, times,
                  serif;
25          letter-spacing: 1px;
26          font-weight: normal;      }
27
28   h1      {    font-size: 2.5em;    }
29   h2      {    font-size: 2em;      }
30   h3      {    font-size: 1.25em;   }
31   h4, h5, h6 { font-size: 1em; }
32   p       {
33          text-align: left;
34          font-size: .75em;
35          margin: 5px 0;
36          line-height: 1.5; }
37   blockquote {
38          font-size: .75em;
39          margin: 10px 0;
40          padding: 10px 0;
41          border-top: 1px solid rgb(128,128,128);
42          border-bottom: 1px solid rgb(128,128,128);
43          line-height: 1; }
44   li      {
45          font-size: .75em;
46          margin: 2px 0;      }

47   /*--------------------------------------------------------
48          Grid
49   ----------------------------------------------------*/
50   #page {
51          position: relative;
52          display: block;
53          margin:0 auto;
54          width: 980px;
55
56          _width: 960px;      }
57   /*--------------------------------------------------------
58          Grid - Rows
59   ----------------------------------------------------*/
60   .row {
61          position: relative;
62          display: block;
63          margin:0 auto;      }
64   #header  {    height: 100px;       }
65   #content {    padding-top: 20px; }
66   #footer  {    height: 20px;        }
67   /*--------------------------------------------------------
68          Grid - Columns
69   ----------------------------------------------------*/
70   .column {
71          position: relative;
72          display: block;
73          float: left;      }
74   .alignclear        {     clear: both; }
75   #aside1 {
76          top: 60px;
77          left: -80px;
78          width: 314px;       }
79   #article1 {
80          left: -40px;
81          width: 470px;       }
82   #aside2 {     width: 190px;        }
83   /*--------------------------------------------------------
84          Grid - Sections
85   ----------------------------------------------------*/
86   .section {
87          position: relative;
88          display: block;            }
89   #header .search {
90          position: absolute;
91          right: 10px;
92          top: 10px;    }
93   #footer .copyright {
94          margin: 0 20px;
95          float: left; }
96
97   #aside1 .section  {
98          width: 100%;
99          padding-bottom: 60px;      }
```

Build *continued*

Prototype: Combining Style Sheets

Style sheets can be linked to or imported into the HTML as detailed in Chapter 5, "Semantics," in the "Where to Put Style Rules" section. There are two basic strategies for external style sheets, each with its strengths and weaknesses:

All In One

Place all of your CSS code into a single file. From an optimization standpoint, this is your best bet, as it takes only a single download to get all of the code. The downside is that this can mean a lot of extra code per page, and conflicts between styles are more likely.

Pros

- Allows user agent to cache one file that can then be reused without extra required download time.

- Due to predictable nature, less likely to cause unforeseen style conflicts.

Cons

- Greatly limits design flexibility between channels and projects. Difficult to edit and override styles.

- Will most likely lead to Web developer kludges to overcome shortcomings.

Modular Library

A library of CSS files allows you to break down the code by function. Each function has its own unique file that can be indepen-
dently edited and then imported into a single external CSS file
that is in turn linked to an HTML page. Every page will have a
unique external CSS file, but that file will be composed of multiple imported CSS files.

Pros

☞ Easy to edit.

☞ Cuts down on unnecessary code.

☞ Each external file is cached separately and so will be reused as
needed without additional download required.

Cons

☞ Requires a server call for each imported style sheet, slowing
initial download.

☞ IE has some difficulties loading external style sheets using
@import before the page content loads.

Deploy

Once you have built your prototype pages, you are ready to populate them with their initial content and begin getting reactions.

Alpha

Your Web site is not ready for prime time (and is possibly password protected), but you can share it with people you know and trust to give you honest feedback and constructive criticism. Make sure the feedback comes with the following information:

- The exact URL where the problem occurred.
- The visitor's browser, version, and operating system.
- Where possible, a screen grab showing the problem.

Beta

Sometimes called the "soft launch," beta launches are becoming increasingly popular as a way to avoid criticism for any bugs on the site after it goes public. Generally the site is made available to the public but not promoted. Prominent feedback functionality should be provided to report any problems.

Launch

It's time for the hard launch, but don't let that stop you from making improvements.

Iterate

Design is an iterative process, where new ideas and new concepts should constantly be explored to make improvements. The Web makes the job of iteration easy because the means of distribution are instantaneous. You can make changes and publish them at the speed of light (or at least at the speed of your Internet connection).

Iteration is not something you do at the end of the process; it is an integral part of the entire process. Always be willing to question your assumptions throughout the process whenever new facts present themselves.

Design iteration can cause friction on a project, as project managers and developers are generally more comfortable with a linear process. This takes you back into planning: The more you can show the benefits of particular changes in your documentation, the smoother it is in convincing the rest of the team to go along.

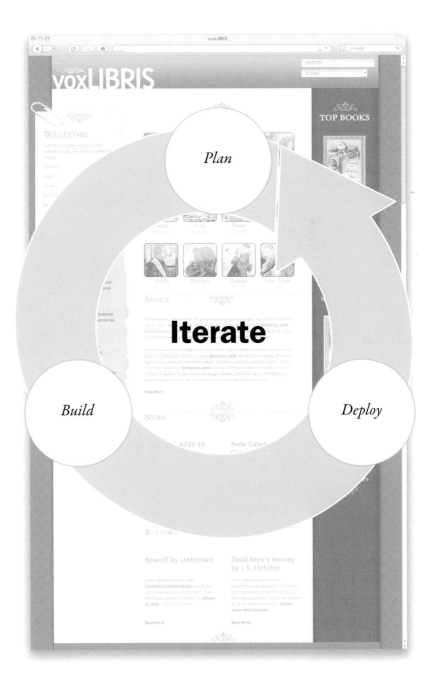

Plan

Build

Iterate

Deploy

The Grid System

The ultimate resource in grid systems.

" The grid system is an aid, not a guarantee. It permits a number of possible uses and each designer can look for a solution appropriate to his personal style. But one must learn how to use the grid; it is an art that requires practice. "
Josef Müller-Brockmann

Articles

Quiet Structure
Quiet structure is achieved when you de—emphasize the structural elements and bring a rhythmical consistency to the layout.
04.May.2009

Columns & Grids
Article on Mezzoblue exploring the different column options for grid based designs.
20.Apr.2009

Cutting and Sewing Grid-Based Design
Discusses the steps taken when measuring and cutting a comp layed over a grid and turning that data into CSS.
07.Apr.2009

View All Articles →

Tools

Grid System Generator
The grid system generator will create fixed grid systems in valid css/xhtml for rapid prototyping, development and production.
04.May.2009

Grid Calculator 10% Discount
Special 10% discount on Grid Calculator for TGS readers. Offer only valid this week: 4/27 - 5/1. Enter in the following code upon checkout : Baseline.
26.Apr.2009

Variable Grid System
The variable grid system is a quick way to generate an underlying CSS grid for your site. The CSS generated file is based on the 960 Grid System.
20.Apr.2009

View All Tools →

Books

The Grid Book
Examines the history of ten grids that changed the world and charts the evolution of each.
07.Apr.2009

Layout Essentials: 100 Design Principles for Using Grids
This book outlines and demonstrate basic layout/grid guidelines and rules through 100 entries.
23.Mar.2009

A Type Primer
A Type Primer provides a practical guide for beginners, presenting the basic principles and applications of typography. The book includes a section on how type is applied to a grid.
18.Feb.2009

View All Books →

Templates

InDesign 568x792 Grid System (12)
By Dario Galvagno. Adobe InDesign file with a grid system for a 568pts x 792pts page that is divided into 12 columns and rows using the Golden Ratio. Includes a 12pt baseline grid.
16.Apr.2009

Illustrator 974px Grid System (12)
By Neil Bradley. Adobe Illustrator file with a grid system for a 974px wide page that is divided into 12 columns and rows using the Rule of Thirds (Golden Ratio). Includes a 16px baseline grid.
18.Feb.2009

InDesign A4 Complex Grid System (12)
Adobe InDesign file with a grid system based on Karl Gerstner's work for Capital Magazine. The grid features a 4, 6 or 12 column and a 4 or 6 row setup.
09.Feb.2009

View All Templates →

Blog

5 Column Grid Typeface
A typeface designed on a 5 column grid as a framework for building a modular font family.
04.May.2009

Warm Forest Templates
Flash based templates that are designed with a strong focus on typography, grids and usability.
20.Apr.2009

Grid Based Clock Screensaver
A Grid-Based-Clock-Screensaver for OS X created by Build.
11.Mar.2009

View All Blog Posts →

Inspiration

Ace Jet 170
AisleOne
Athletics
BBDK
Blanka
Build
Corporate Risk Watch
David Airey
Design Assembly
Dirty Mouse
Experimenta
Experimental Jetset
Form Fifty Five
Grafik Magazine
Grain Edit
Graphic Hug
I Love Typography
Lamosca
magCulture
Mark Boulton
Minimal Sites
Monocle
Neubau
NewWork
OK-RM
Original Linkage
Robin Uleman
SampsonMay
Schmid Today
September Industry
Souleilis
Subtraction
Swiss Legacy
Thinking for a Living
This Studio
Toko
Typographic Posters
Visuelle
Xavier Encinas
Year of the Sheep

About
Made popular by the International Typographic Style movement and pioneered by legends like Josef Müller-Brockmann and Wim Crouwel, the grid is the foundation of any solid design. The Grid System is an ever-growing resource where graphic designers can learn about grid systems, the golden ratio and baseline grids.

Created by **Antonio Carusone**, graphic designer and author of the design and typography blog **AisleOne**. Special thanks to **Duane King** for his help and wisdom.

If you want to say hi or for general inquiries, send an email to: **hello@thegridsystem.org**

Have an article, tool, template or news you want to submit? Send an email to: **submit@thegridsystem.org**

Subscribe
Want to stay updated with the most recent content? Subscribe below via email for daily updates or to the RSS feed.

Subscribe by Email
Subscribe to RSS

4107 readers
BY FEEDBURNER

Archives
May 2009
April 2009
March 2009
February 2009
January 2009
December 2008
November 2008

Goodies
LegiStyles
AisleOne Store
Wallpapers
The Grid System Group
Inter-Typo-Style Group
Wim Crouwel Group

Colophon
Made on a **Mac**
Set in **Helvetica**
Themed in **Futorosity**
Hosted by **Media Temple**
Powered by **Wordpress**

Designers Bookshop | **Thinking For A Living** | **You Work For Them**

Grids are a time-honored method for creating strong visual designs with hierarchy, visual rhythm, and context. Although CSS is not explicitly set up for creating grids—there are no row or column properties—designers have developed methods to overcome this limitation.

The voxLibris site is designed around a three-column structure with a fixed width and fluid height. We'll start by resetting all of the browser default properties, and then creating a layout grid for our design.

CHAPTER 8

LAYOUT

Structure

Layout begins with the HTML document, which creates the structure on which the CSS is applied. A Web page's structure can take a variety of forms and will depend greatly on the type of site you are creating. Still, many Web pages have structural elements in common. Along with the markup that sets content elements such as headers, paragraphs, lists, links, and forms; we'll add certain IDs and classes that will be used to define those structural elements.

The Grid System

thegridsystem.org

Everything you ever wanted to know about designing with a grid (and more). It even includes an onion skin layer you can toggle on and off to see the site's own grid.

Head and Body

The HTML for all Web pages is split into two main blocks set off by tags:

01   *<head>*: The head is where all the meta information about the Web page is placed—information about the page, such as its title, author, and description. None of this information is displayed in the browser window itself. This is also the best place to put the CSS that will be applied to the body of the page.

02   *<body>*: All Web pages exist within the body of the browser window, which is the eventual parent of all elements on the page. By setting styles with the body HTML selector, you also set default styles for every element on the page (except for some form elements). This is where you set the background that fills the entire browser window.

voxLIBRIS

Welcome

voxLIBRIS provides public domain
audiobooks you can download free of
charge.

GENRES

ABOUT

NEWS

REVIEWS

DONATE

CONTACT

Top 50 WTF Comic Moments
Countdown The Most Outrageous
Moments In Comic Book History!
www.UGO.com/Comics

HP Global Citizenship
Why Protecting Privacy is Essential
For Socially Responsible
Companies
www.hp.com

Environments
Find Environments & More
Environments Options Here!
Octopedia.com

Ads by Oogle

GENRES

Adventure
34 books

Anthropology
34 books

Children
34 books

Epic
34 books

Fantasy
34 books

History
34 books

Humor
34 books

Medical
34 books

Mystery
34 books

Philosophy
34 books

Romance
34 books

Science Fiction
34 books

About

Nulla sed felis. Sed et tellus. Vivamus venenatis suscipit magna. Vestibulum hendrerit
iaculis nunc. Morbi posuere tempus elit. Ut commodo mattis nisl. dictum ac, ante
Vestibulum tortor.Vivamus elit. Nam nisi felis, egestas et, varius in, suscipit at, risus.
Lorem ipsum dolor sit amet, consectetur adipiscing elit. Sed eget sapien.

Suspendisse aliquam suscipit elit. Sed a lorem. Suspendisse fermentum dolor in nibh
dignissim bibendum. Etiam a eros et dictum ac, ante odio dapibus tempus. Phasellus
ligula. Donec venenatis hendrerit tellus. Vestibulum dapibus augue et augue. Nulla
imperdiet. Maecenas dictum ac, ante sed erat id neque lobortis elementum. Proin
eleifend magna ac turpis. Curabitur magna sapien, convallis vitae, imperdiet non, sagittis
aliquam, tellus. Nunc pretium orci cursus nisl facilisis pulvinar.

Read More

News

voxLIBRIS Adds 30 New Books

Lorem ipsum dolor sit amet,
consectetur adipiscing elit. Vestibulum
commodo metus sit amet libero. Cras
nisl neque, lacinia id, mollis vel, dictum
ac, ante. Vestibulum tortor.

Read More

New Categories Coming Next Month

Lorem ipsum dolor sit amet,
consectetur adipiscing elit. Vestibulum
commodo metus sit amet libero. Cras
nisl neque, lacinia id, mollis vel, dictum
ac, ante. Vestibulum tortor. Lorem
ipsum dolor sit amet.

Read More

Reviews

Bowolf by Unknown

Lorem ipsum dolor sit amet,
consectetur adipiscing elit. Vestibulum
commodo metus sit amet libero. Cras
nisl neque, lacinia id, mollis vel, dictum
ac, ante. Vestibulum tortor.

Read More

Dead Men's Money by J.S. Fletcher

Lorem ipsum dolor sit amet,
consectetur adipiscing elit. Vestibulum
commodo metus sit amet libero. Cras
nisl neque, lacinia id, mollis vel, dictum
ac, ante. Vestibulum tortor. Lorem
ipsum dolor sit amet.

Read More

TOP BOOKS

Through the Looking Glass
by Lewis Carol

Princess of Mars
by Edgar Rice Burroughs

Through the Looking Glass
by Aesop

Gods of Mars
by Edgar Rice Burroughs

Structure *continued*

The HTML Framework for CSS

A framework is a standard set of IDs and classes added to a Web page's HTML to facilitate common page components, which can then be referenced in the CSS. Although the exact framework may vary from site to site, these are the most common frameworks:

- **Page** (08): Controls whether the grid is fluid or fixed. Setting an absolute width and/or height fixes the page's flow vertically or horizontally.

- **Rows** (09, 10, 32): Horizontal elements within the grid, stacked from top to bottom and stretching the width of the page element.

- **Columns** (11, 16, 27): Vertical elements within the grid, stacked next to each other from left to right and stretching the height of its row.

- **Sections** (12, 13, 17, 20, 22, 24, 28): Blocks within the grid containing content and functionality.

voxLIBRIS

search
[video   ▾]

Welcome

voxLIBRIS provides public domain audiobooks you can download free of charge.

- Genres
- About
- News
- Reviews
- Donate
- Contact

Top 50 WTF Comic Moments
Countdown The Most Outrageous Moments In Comic Book History!
www.UGO.com/Comics

HP Global Citizenship
Why Protecting Privacy is Essential For Socially Responsible Companies
www.hp.com

Environments
Find Environments & More Environments Options Here!
Octopedia.com

Ads by Oogle

Genres

- Adventure 34 books
- Anthropology 12 books
- Children 90 books
- Epic 6 books
- Fantasy 13 books
- History 46 books
- Humor 18 books
- Medical 21 books
- Mystery 67 books
- Philosophy 2 books
- Romance 103 books
- SciFi 54 books

About

Mollis sed felis. Sed at tellus. Vivamus convallis convisit magna. Vestibulum hendrerit iaculis arcu. Morbi pos nunc tempus elit. Ut commodo turpis nisi, dictum eu, orto.

The code shown has had all content stripped out to show the HTML framework. For the full code listing, see Appendix A.

Note that without any CSS applied to the page the browser default styles are still applied, which we will need to deal with.

```
01  <!DOCTYPE html PUBLIC "-//W3C//DTD
       XHTML 1.0 Strict//EN" "http://www.
       w3.org/TR/xhtml1/DTD/xhtml1-strict.
       dtd">
02  <html xmlns="http://www.w3.org/1999/xhtml">
03  <head>
04      <title>voxLIBRIS</title>
05      <link href="_css/main.css" rel="stylesheet"
           type="text/css" media="all"/>
06  </head>
07  <body>
08  <div id="page">
09      <div id="header" class="row"></div>
10      <div id="content" class="row">
11        <div id="aside1" class="column">
12          <div id="navigationmain"
             class="section navigation"></div>
13          <div id="ads01" class="section ads"></
             div>
14        </div>
15      </div>
16      <div id="article1" class="column">
17        <div id="genrelist" class="section">
18          <br class="alignclear" />
19        </div>
20        <div id="about" class="section">
21            <br class="alignclear" /></div>
22        <div id="news" class="section">
23            <br class="alignclear" /></div>
24        <div id="news" class="section">
25            <br class="alignclear" /></div>
26      </div>
27      <div id="aside2" class="column">
28        <div id="topbooks" class="section
             topbooks">
29            <br class="alignclear"/></div>
30        </div>
31        <br class="alignclear" />
32        <div id="footer" class="row">
33          <br class="alignclear" /></div>
34      </div>
35    </div>
36  </body>
37  </html>
```

Structure *continued*

Adding CSS

Different strategies for adding external style sheets are detailed in Chapter 7, "Designing with CSS" in the "Prototype: Combining Style Sheets" section.

voxLibris will use the modular library approach to adding external style sheets. The idea is to set up several external files based on use and import them into a single CSS file, which then gets linked to the target HTML file. This gives you the versatility to quickly change one part of the design or interface simply by swapping style sheets.

For voxLibris, we're using four distinct style sheets:

- *default.css*: Resets the browser default styles and sets the site-wide default styles. This style sheet is detailed later in this chapter.

- *layout.css*: Defines the grid structure and layout for the page. This style sheet is detailed later in this chapter.

- *navigation.css*: Provides user interface styles, such as links, navigation, and buttons.

- *chrome.css*: Adds the graphic layer to the design, including backgrounds, logos, and design flourishes.

main.css imports all of the external style sheets used in the page, and then links to *index.html*.

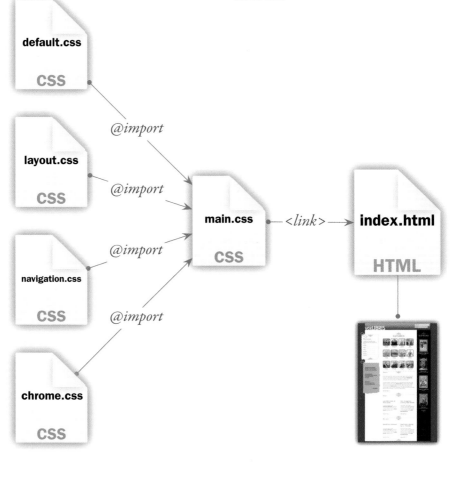

```
01   /*----------------------------------------------------------
02        Imported Styles
03   ----------------------------------------------------------*/
04   @import url("default.css");
05   @import url("layout.css");
06   @import url("navigation.css");
07   @import url("chrome.css");
```

Default Styles

It's an important fact of life with CSS that, once a style is set, it's set not only for the particular HTML tag it's being applied to, but to all tags within that tag as well. To make adding new styles as easy as possible, there are two default styles that you need to know.

Resetting Browser Default Styles

Load a Web page into a browser, and even before you add any CSS to the page, you will notice that the page already has a very rough style to it: headlines are bolder and larger, links are colored and underlined, lists are indented with bullets, and paragraphs have margins. These are the browser default styles that I discussed in Chapter 5, "Semantics" in the "Inheritance" section. In the absence of overriding styles from CSS, these default styles are applied. It's helpful to reset the default styles for all of your HTML tags to get more consistent results across browser types.

Setting Your Default Styles

Set the specific default styles for the HTML tags you will use in your designs. This sets the baseline styles particular to your site and will be used unless overridden by specific styles later in your CSS.

voxLIBRIS

search
titles [Go]

Welcome

voxLIBRIS provides public domain audiobooks you can download free of charge

Genres
About
News
Reviews
Donate
Contact

Top 10 WTF Comic Moments
Countdown The Most Outrageous Moments In Comic Book History!
www.UUU.com/Comics

U2 Global Citizenship
Why Protecting Privacy is Essential For Socially Responsible Companies
www.hp.com

Environments
Find Environments & More Environments Options Here!
3classedia.com

Ads by Google

Genres

Adventure 34 books
Anthropology 17 books
Children 96 books
Epic 6 books
Fantasy 13 books
History 48 books
Humor 18 books
Medical 11 books
Mystery 67 books
Philosophy 2 books
Romance 103 books
SciFi 54 books

About

Nulla sed felis. Sed et tellus. Vivamus venenatis suscipit magna. Vestibulum hendrerit iaculis nunc. Morbi posuere tempus elit. Ut commodo mattis nisl. **dictum ac, ante.** Vestibulum tortor.Vivamus elit. Nam nisl felis, egestas et, varius in, suscipit at, risus. Lorem ipsum dolor sit amet, consectetur adipiscing elit. Sed eget sapien.

Suspendisse aliquam suscipit elit. Sed a lorem. Suspendisse fermentum dolor in nibh dignissim bibendum. Etiam a eros et **dictum ac, ante** odio dapibus tempus. Phasellus ligula. Donec venenatis hendrerit tellus. Vestibulum dapibus augue et augue. Nulla imperdiet. Maecenas **dictum ac, ante** sed erat id neque lobortis elementum. Proin eleifend magna ac turpis. Curabitur magna sapien, convallis vitae, imperdiet non, sagittis aliquam, tellus. Nunc pretium orci cursus nisl facilisis pulvinar.

Read More

News

*vox*LIBRIS Adds 30 New Books

Lorem ipsum dolor sit amet, **consectetur adipiscing elit.** Vestibulum commodo metus ut amet libero. Cras nisi neque, lacinia id, mollis vel, **dictum ac, ante.** Vestibulum tortor

Read More

New Categories Coming Next Month

Browser styles have been replaced with default styles, including margins, padding, and basic typography (see Chapter 9).

```
01  /*------------------------------------------------------
02        Reset Browser Inherited Styles
03  ------------------------------------------------------*/
04  html, body, div, span, applet, object, iframe, h1, h2,
        h3, h4, h5, h6, p, blockquote, pre, a, abbr,
        acronym, address, big, cite, code, del, dfn, em,
        font, img, ins, kbd, q, s, samp, small, strike,
        strong, sub, sup, tt, var, dd, dl, dt, li, ol, ul,
        fieldset, form, label, legend, table, caption,
        tbody, tfoot, thead, tr, th, td {
05        margin: 0;
06        padding: 0;
07        border: 0;
08        outline: 0;
09        background: none;
10        font-weight: inherit;
11        font-style: inherit;
12        font-family: inherit;
13        font-size: 100%;
14        text-align: left;
15        line-height: 1;
16        vertical-align: baseline;
17        list-style: none;        }
```

```
18  /*------------------------------------------------------
19        Default Styles
20  ------------------------------------------------------*/
21  body, input, select {
22        color: rgb(105,105,105);
23        font-family: "fontin sans", optima,
              "trebuchet-MS", sans-serif;        }
24  body {background: rgb(0,50,75)
              url(../_images/bg-body.png) repeat 0 0; }
25  h1, h2, h3, h4, h5, h6 {
26        color: rgb(128,128,128);
27        font-family: garamond, cochin, times, serif;
28        letter-spacing: 1px;
29        font-weight: normal;        }
30  h1    {    font-size: 2.5em;    }
31  h2    {    font-size: 2em;      }
32  h3    {    font-size: 1.25em;   }
33  p     {
34        font-size: .75em;
35        margin: 5px 0;
36        line-height: 1.5; }
37  blockquote {
38        font-size: .75em;
39        margin: 10px 0;
40        padding: 10px 0;
41        border-top: 1px solid rgb(128,128,128);
42        border-bottom: 1px solid rgb(128,128,128); }
43  li    {    font-size: .75em;    }
```

The Grid

A simple grid structure uses the HTML framework for CSS to lay out the page. voxLibris uses page, header, footer, and content, but other grid sections might be used as defined in the wire frames while planning the site.

Fluid and fixed grid layouts are discussed in Chapter 7, "Designing with CSS" in the "Page Flow" section.

When you planned your design, one of the first things you needed to decide was whether you would use a fluid or fixed layout. voxLibris uses a fixed width of 980px, so we set that as the width using the *page* ID (04). If we wanted to make this page fluid, we would set the width as a percentage or use max/min widths.

Rows

The *<div>* tags used to create each row will include the row class and a row ID with specific styles.

- Create the row class and then IDs for individual rows based on purpose (header, content, footer).

For the fix to dealing with padding in IE6, read the "Box Model Problem in IE6" section in Chapter 6.

- Be careful when using padding with grid elements, since padding will throw the dimensions off in IE6. If padding is added to an axis that does not have an absolute length set, there is no problem. If the axis does have an absolute length set, though, then IE will shrink the box to accommodate the padding.

- To center a grid element within its parent, set the left/right margin to auto. This puts equal space on both sides of the page, centering it in the browser window.

The three grid rows: header, content, and footer.

voxLIBRIS

Genres

Top Books

Welcome

Adventure 34 books
Anthropology 12 books
Children 98 books
Epic 6 books
Fantasy 13 books
History 45 books
Humor 18 books
Medival 31 books
Mystery 87 books
Philosophy 3 books
Romance 103 books
SciFi 54 books

About

News
voxLIBRIS Adds 30
New Books

New Categories
Coming Next Month

Reviews
Bowolf by Unknown

Dead Men's Money by
J.S. Fletcher

© voxLIBRIS

```
01   /*------------------------------------------------
02       Grid
03   ------------------------------------------------*/
04   #page {
05       position: relative;
06       display: block;
07       margin:0 auto;
08       width: 980px;        }
```

```
09   /*------------------------------------------------
10       Grid - Rows
11   ------------------------------------------------*/
12   .row {
13       position: relative;
14       display: block;
15       margin:0 auto;       }
16   #header {    height: 100px;     }
17   #content {   padding-top: 20px; }
18   #footer {    height: 20px;      }
```

219

The Grid *continued*

Columns

Columns are used to establish a vertical rhythm within the page, allowing you to present information from left to right and make better use of screen real estate.

- Although it may seem counter-intuitive, columns are created by floating block elements next to each other. This lines the blocks up horizontally next to each other.

- As with other grid elements, set the position property for all columns so that child elements will position themselves from the column's origin (top left corner).

- If a column has a specific width, avoid applying padding. If you must use padding, make sure to accommodate IE6 as detailed in "Box Model Problem in IE6" in Chapter 6.

- The *alignclear* class can be added to a *
* tag in your HTML to force columns to drop below, but, more importantly, to also force the column box to the full height of the content.

Why Are My Columns Falling Apart?

Columns will fall apart (dropping underneath each other) if there is not enough width in the page and/or content elements. For example, if the page width is 900px, but the column's width adds up to 901px or more, the far right column will drop below the other columns.

One other note: To break out of the grid, use the position properties (*top*, *right*, *bottom*, and *left*) to move elements from their natural position—potentially even out of their columns.

The three columns: aside1, article1, and aside2

```
19   /*------------------------------------------------------
20          Grid - Columns
21   ------------------------------------------------------*/
22   .column {
23          position: relative;
24          display: block;
25          float: left;   }
26   .alignclear  {      clear: both;  }
27   #aside1 {
28          top: 60px;
29          left: -80px;
30          width: 314px;      }
31   #article1 {
32          left: -40px;
33          width: 470px;      }
34   #aside2 {      width: 190px;      }
```

The Grid *continued*

Sections

Sections (sometimes called modules) are content and functionality blocks within the grid.

- As with other grid elements, set the position property for all sections so that child elements will position themselves from the column's origin (top left corner).

- If a section has a specific width, avoid applying padding. If you must use padding, make sure to accommodate IE6 as detailed in "Box Model Problem in IE6" in Chapter 6.

- Sections can also be floated next to each other and used within columns to create "sub-columns."

Outlines show where sections of the page are located.

```
35  /*---------------------------------------------------------
36      Grid - Sections
37  ---------------------------------------------------------*/
38  .section {
39      position: relative;
40      display: block;           }
41  #aside1 .section {
42      width: 100%;
43      padding-bottom: 60px;   }
44  #aside1 .section h2 {
45      width: 100%;
46      padding: 80px 0 8px 18%;      }
47  #aside1 .section div.content {      width: 100%;      }
48  #aside1 .section p, #aside1 .section ul {
49      width: 65%;
50      margin: 0 auto;
51      margin-bottom: 5px;      }
52  #article1 .section .column {      width: 210px;      }
53  #article1 .section .column+.column {    float: right;  }
54  #article1 .section .column p {      min-height: 110px;}
```

i love typography

APR 21 2009 [37 COMMENTS]

The Typographic Desk Reference

A BRIEF REVIEW

One can never have too many books about type and typography. One of the most recent additions to my own library is Theodore Rosendorf's *The Typographic Desk Reference* or, if you're in a hurry, simply TDR.

From the outset it's worth stressing that this is not a how-to book. It does not compete with Bringhurst's *The Elements of Typographic Style* or Felici's *The Complete Manual of Typography*. It is, as its title makes quite clear, a reference book. Think of it more as a dictionary or rather a pocket encyclopedia of type terms.

Comprising four main sections, it's pretty easy to find your way around — something essential in a book of reference.

Section one, TERMS

A collection of the most important type terms. Definitions are clear and concise, and accompanied by illustrative examples in the margin.

THE TYPOGRAPHIC DESK REFERENCE

m   **transitive**   A serif that flows smoothly out of a main stroke. Transitive serifs are typically *unilateral*. Compare with *reflexive*. *See also* bilateral, reflexive, serif, unilateral, page 97 (diagram).

unilateral   A serif extending to one side of a main stroke. Unilateral serifs can be either *reflexive* or *transitive*. Compare with *bilateral*. *See also* bilateral, serif, reflexive, transitive, page 97 (diagram).

abc ABC   **uppercase**   A font's capital letters. *See also* capitals, lowercase; TERMS: uppercase.

A   **versal**   A dropped or elevated initial capital letter. Also called *initial cap* or *lettrine*. *See also* capitals, drop cap, elevated cap; TERMS: historiated letter.

weight   The heaviness of the stroke for a specific font style, including light, regular, book, medium, demi, bold, extra bold, heavy, black, extra black, etc. *See also* boldface, color/colour, demi.

white line   The blank line between paragraphs. Two hard returns. *See also* GLYPHS: return/carriage return; TERMS: paragraph.

white space   Characters or processes used to create unmarked space within text. Portions of a page left unmarked. *See also* GLYPHS: space; TERMS: spacing.

x-height   The height of lowercase letters without ascenders or descenders. Also called *mean line* or *x-line*. *See also* cap height, lowercase, page 97 (diagram).

ANATOMY & FORM

Popular articles

How to make a font
Best 'fonts' of 2008
Type history series
Web typography guide
On choosing type
Identify that font
From Moleskine to market
Who shot the serif?
Inconspicuous vertical metrics
Sunday type: napkin type

An Event Apart The design conference for people who make websites.

ads via THE DECK

Recent articles

WE love typography
Yes, we kern!
The first one's the hardest
Malabar released
Watchmen, watchtype
Read between the leading
TDC2 2009 results
iFont, iPhone
Chelsea, darling
Helvetica Moleskine
WIT: projected type
On diacritics
The week in type: going green
Inconspicuous vertical metrics
To a typetastic new year
Reminga bold italic
Best 'fonts' of 2008
the week in type — Zócalo
The Type Directors Club
Interview: Seb Lester
Free fonts from FontFont
30 inspiring type treatments
twiT — good type
Printing, 1947 [video]
Footnotes *†‡§
twiT — die neue
Sexy type
twiT — casanova
Vote iLT
Type links roundup
Sunday Type: tomate type

36,553
SUBSCRIBERS VIA RS

APRIL FO

FF Milo Ser
Apertura
Comenius

MARCH FO

BREE Oblique
Plumero
Gotham conc
euroglor

FEBRUARY FO

newt serif
chamber sar

JANUARY FO

kewlscrip
sugarpie
Ff Tisa
Buffet Scrip
Reminga

DECEMBER FO

Mister K
Great circu
Fairbank
Ff trixi
compendium
WEATHERE
WOOD * TYP

The fonts you choose convey as much of your Web site's message as your words. The initial response to a Web page is a visceral one—a reaction to the visual design—rather than a conscious thought. This happens within seconds of the page loading, and beyond the images, chrome, and colors, one of the first things the visitor notices is all of the squiggles making words.

The sad fact is, though, Web typography is mostly boring because the only font families at your disposal (unless you put the text into a graphic) are the typefaces installed on the end user's machine. All this may seem very limiting at first, but it's not nearly as bad as most designers believe.

CHAPTER 9

TYPOGRAPHY

Font Choices

The process of defining the typeface for a particular block of text is relatively straightforward—specify a list of font-family names, separated by commas, with the last name in the list being a generic font family (*serif, sans-serif, monospace, handwritten,* or *fantasy*). If a particular font in the list is not available, the browser moves to the next one, until there is a match.

font-family: georgia, times, "times new roman", sans-serif.

However, the simplicity of setting a typeface belies the complexity of picking the right font to communicate your message.

Core Web Fonts

It is estimated that there are more than 100,000 fonts available electronically. Yet, if you look around the Web, you would be forgiven if you thought there were only three—Arial (Helvetica on the Mac), Times New Roman (Times on the Mac), and Georgia. These are the three most popular fonts because—along with Verdana, Trebuchet MS, Andale Mono, Arial Black, Courier New, Comic Sans MS, Impact, and Webdings—they are the core Web fonts that are widely distributed on Mac and Windows computers. So, you are almost guaranteed that these 11 fonts will be on the end user's machine. Eleven fonts out of tens of thousands. Not very inspiring, is it?

i l o v e   t y p o g r a p h y

ilovetypography.com

If you love typography, this is a great resource on typography for both the Web and print.

Andale Mono

Arial

Arial Black

Courier New

Comic Sans MS

Georgia

Impact

Times New Roman

Trebuchet MS

Verdana

Webdings

Font Choices *continued*

Web-Safe Fonts

For a complete list of the Web-Safe fonts with samples, check out speaking-in-styles. com/typography/web-safe-fonts.

The 11 core Web fonts are installed almost universally on all computers. However, there are many other fonts commonly installed on the end user's computer that are commonly overlooked. These fonts can be safely employed in your designs, using CSS:

01 **Operating system fonts**: All operating systems come with pre-installed fonts. In addition to the core Web fonts, Windows XP adds 9 typefaces, Windows Vista adds another 7 (16 total), and Mac OS X supplies a whopping 30 fonts.

02 **Microsoft Office fonts**: The one application almost universally installed on all computers is Microsoft Office. Love it or hate it, Microsoft Office 2007 has another 121 fonts, while its Mac equivalent (Office 2008) includes 68 fonts. Even better, the Windows and Mac lists have 62 fonts in common.

03 **iLife fonts**: All Macs (consumer and Pro) have Apple iLife pre-installed, which has 13 fonts pre-installed.

That makes a total of 148 fonts likely to be on a given Windows box and 120 fonts on Macs, with an overlap of 73 fonts.

A Font by Any Other Name...

We often use the word "font" indiscriminately when what we really mean is font family or typeface. A font is actually the complete character set of a single size and style of a particular typeface. However, because the broader meaning is commonly used to mean typeface, let's just keep it that way. Keep in mind that when you are defining the font property in CSS, you are defining the weight, style, variations, and size in addition to the font family.

Andale Mono

Arial Narrow

Arial Rounded MT Bold

Baskerville Old Face

Bauhaus 93

Bell MT

Bernard MT Condensed

Book Antiqua

Bookman Old Style

Bradley Hand ITC TT

Britannic Bold

Brush Script MT

Calibri

Calisto MT

Cambria

Candara

Century

Century Gothic

Century Schoolbook

Colonna MT

Consolas

Constantia

Cooper Black

COPPERPLATE GOTHIC BOLD

COPPERPLATE GOTHIC LIGHT

Corbel

Courier New

Curlz MT

Edwardian Script ITC

ENGRAVERS MT

Footlight MT Light

Franklin Gothic Book

Franklin Gothic Medium

Garamond

Gill Sans MT

Gill Sans Ultra Bold

Gloucester MT Extra Condensed

Goudy Old Style

Haettenschweiler

Harrington

Imprint MT Shadow

Lucida Bright

Lucida Calligraphy

Lucida Console

Lucida Fax

Lucida Sans

Lucida Sans Typewriter

Lucida Sans Unicode

Mistral

MS Mincho

MS Reference Sans Serif

Onyx

Papyrus

Perpetua

PERPETUA TITLING MT

Playbill

Rockwell

Rockwell Extra Bold

STENCIL

Tahoma

Tw Cen MT

Wide Latin

Font Choices *continued*

Downloadable Fonts

The holy grail of Web typography is downloadable fonts. After all, Adobe Flash allows you to use any font at your disposal in your design by embedding the font in the SWF file. Why can't we just download a font file (like we do an image file) to be used by CSS? The short answer is, surprisingly, *we can*, or at least CSS has the grammar to allow exactly that.

Using the *@fontface* rule you can set the source of a font file and give it a unique name for use within your designs. For example, placing

@font-face { font-family: "fontin sans";
src: url(fonts/Fontin_Sans_R_45b.otf);}

at the top of your CSS imports the Open Type font *Fontin_ Sans_R_45b.otf*, which can be referenced in the CSS as *fontin sans*.

Before you get too excited, though, currently, only Sa3.1+ supports the downloading of the common font formats True Type (.ttf) and Open Type (.otf). Although both Op and FF have plans to add support, the big holdout it is IE. What could Microsoft possibly have against downloadable fonts? To understand their reasoning, you would first have to understand the vagaries of end user license agreements (EULA) and intellectual property (IP). Still, you can support downloadable fonts in your designs as long as you are willing to think fluidly about your typography.

How Fast Are Downloadable Fonts?

A font file is a file, so it has to be downloaded, which can affect performance. Currently there is no way to subset fonts (just download the needed glyphs to render the page), but the font will be cached, so once downloaded for one page, it's available for other pages much more quickly.

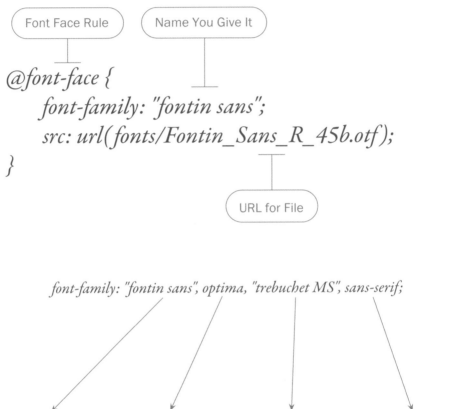

Fluid Typography

At first, Web typography can seem stiflingly limited, with few typestyles to choose from and limited controls. This is especially true if you are a designer who wants your results to look exactly like in your visual comps. If you are willing to think more fluidly about your typography, though, giving up some control, you will find more alternatives.

As discussed in the previous section, we have three main sources for fonts—core Web fonts, Web-safe fonts, and downloadable fonts. The advantage of CSS is that we can choose any or all of these sources and specify a list of fonts to be used, depending on the end user's setup.

In the example, the font Fontin Sans is downloaded with Web-safe font backup of Optima, a core Web font backup of Trebuchet MS, and a final generic font backup of Sans-Serif.

For the level 1 header, I'm using Garamond from the Web-safe font list, Times from the core Web fonts list, and Serif as the generic font.

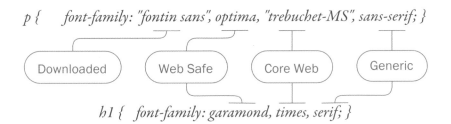

Fluid Typography *continued*

Choosing Typefaces

Although fluid typography frees you to try different typefaces, there are a few important ideas to keep in mind while putting together your font-family list:

- Choose fonts that are as visually similar as possible.

- For headline copy, use fonts with similar widths and kerning. Headlines generally have a finite space they can fill (one or two lines), so it's important that the typefaces you choose run roughly the same length.

- For body copy, select fonts with bold, italic, and bold/italic versions. Fonts that do not have specific weight and style versions will be synthesized by the browser, which is generally not as attractive as a true version.

- If you use a downloaded font and/or a Web-safe font, always include core Web fonts and generic font families as backups. Most browsers will not support downloadable fonts, and some computers may not have the Web-safe font you chose.

- Finally, test the fonts in different combinations. If you use different font families in different selectors, make sure all of the fonts work well together, since you can never predict which two will be used.

Welcome   *Fontin Sans*

Welcome   *Optima*

Welcome   *Trebuchet-MS*

Fontin Sans	*Optima*	*Trebuchet-MS*
Lorem ipsum dolor sit amet, **consectetur** adipiscing elit. *Vestibulum* commodo metus sit amet libero. Cras nisl neque, lacinia id, ***mollis vel***, dictum ac, ante. Vestibulum tortor dui, convallis a, dapibus vitae, volutpat nec, justo. Integer dui.	Lorem ipsum dolor sit amet, **consectetur** adipiscing elit. *Vestibulum* commodo metus sit amet libero. Cras nisl neque, lacinia id, ***mollis vel***, dictum ac, ante. Vestibulum tortor dui, convallis a, dapibus vitae, volutpat nec, justo. Integer dui.	Lorem ipsum dolor sit amet, **consectetur** adipiscing elit. *Vestibulum* commodo metus sit amet libero. Cras nisl neque, lacinia id, ***mollis vel***, dictum ac, ante. Vestibulum tortor dui, convallis a, dapibus vitae, volutpat nec, justo. Integer dui.

p {   font-family: "fontin sans" optima, "trebuchet-MS", sans-serif; }

Sizing Text in CSS

Although you can set your font size using a variety of units, the most versatile method is to set the font size to 100% in the body tag (which uses the browser's default size as its basis) and then use ems to set the specific font sizes for individual elements as needed. Using ems will set font size relative to one another and parent elements, meaning that the page will scale up and down gracefully if the user zooms in and out.

Most browsers (with the exception of IE6) now accommodate font sizes set in pixels when zooming in and out, so, if you are not into doing the math to keep up with using ems, you are increasingly safe using pixels.

Jos Buivenga provides nine excellent fonts that you can use as downloadable fonts on your Web site. I used Fontin Sans as an example for the voxLibris site.

Styling Text

Because styles are inherited, the first place to set your default typographic styles (or to change them from the browser defaults) is in the body, input, and select HTML selectors. This will set your defaults over the entire page, so you will only need to set these properties again if you want to change them for a specific element.

Headers

Headers are commonly differentiated through font family, color, size, and weight. You might also want to add some letter or word spacing , but use those styles sparingly—a little goes a long way.

01   When setting header styles, it's best to set all of the common styles first (05).

02   Set differentiating styles (usually size) for each individually (10–13).

03   Set styles for specific instances using contextual styles—for example, how the level 2 header should be treated if it's in column 1 rather than column 3 (14).

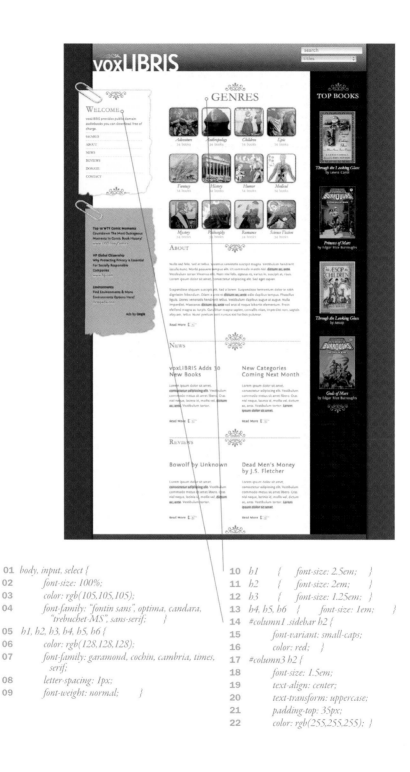

```
01  body, input, select {
02       font-size: 100%;
03       color: rgb(105,105,105);
04       font-family: "fontin sans", optima, candara,
             "trebuchet-MS", sans-serif;    }
05  h1, h2, h3, h4, h5, h6 {
06       color: rgb(128,128,128);
07       font-family: garamond, cochin, cambria, times,
             serif;
08       letter-spacing: 1px;
09       font-weight: normal;        }

10  h1      {   font-size: 2.5em;     }
11  h2      {   font-size: 2em;       }
12  h3      {   font-size: 1.25em;    }
13  h4, h5, h6   {    font-size: 1em;      }
14  #column1 .sidebar h2 {
15       font-variant: small-caps;
16       color: red;      }
17  #column3 h2 {
18       font-size: 1.5em;
19       text-align: center;
20       text-transform: uppercase;
21       padding-top: 35px;
22       color: rgb(255,255,255);  }
```

Styling Text *continued*

Paragraph and Block Quotes

If you set your base styles in the body HTML selector, generally there's not a lot of work to do for the paragraph tags (*<p>*) and block quote (*<blockquote>*) tags.

- For **paragraphs**, you may want to make the text a bit smaller than the standard, set margins above and below, and I always recommend opening up the line height to at least 1.25 line spacing (125%) or higher.

- For **block quotes**, you may also want to set a border, background color, or background image to set the quote off from other text on the page.

Lists

You can also use the list tag to create a menu or controls, as shown in Chapter 10, "Navigation."

Typographically, lists are indented and often have a lower line height than paragraphs. Additional, you can set the bullet style, either choosing one of the predefined bullet styles or creating your own image for the bullet. You might think that using the list-image property is the easiest way to do that, but that's not common practice. Using a background image gives a lot more versatility.

```
01  p      {
02         text-align: left;
03         font-size: .75em;
04         margin: 5px 0;
05         line-height: 1.5; }
06  blockquote {
07         font-size: .75em;
08         margin: 10px 0;
09         border: 1px solid rgb(128,128,128);
10         line-height: 1; }
```

Nulla sed felis. Sed et tellus. Vivamus venenatis suscipit magna. Vestibulum hendrerit iaculis nunc. Morbi posuere tempus elit. Ut commodo mattis nisi. **dictum ac, ante**. Vestibulum tortor.Vivamus elit. Nam nisi felis, egestas et, varius in, suscipit at, risus. Lorem ipsum dolor sit amet, consectetur adipiscing elit. Sed eget sapien.

Suspendisse aliquam suscipit elit. Sed a lorem. Suspendisse fermentum dolor in nibh dignissim bibendum. Etiam a eros et **dictum ac, ante** odio dapibus tempus. Phasellus ligula. Donec venenatis hendrerit tellus. Vestibulum dapibus augue at augue. Nulla imperdiet. Maecenas **dictum ac, ante** sed erat id neque lobortis elementum. Proin eleifend magna ac turpis. Curabitur magna sapien, convallis vitae, imperdiet non, sagittis aliquam, tellus. Nunc pretium orci cursus nisl facilisis pulvinar.

Suspendisse aliquam suscipit elit. Sed a lorem. Suspendisse fermentum dolor in nibh dignissim bibendum. Etiam a eros et dictum ac, ante odio dapibus tempus. Phasellus ligula. Donec venenatis hendrerit tellus. Vestibulum dapibus augue at augue. Nulla imperdiet. Maecenas sed erat id neque lobortis elementum. Proin eleifend magna ac turpis. Curabitur magna sapien, convallis vitae, imperdiet non, sagittis aliquam, tellus. Nunc pretium orci cursus nisl facilisis pulvinar.

```
01  li     {
02         font-size: .75em;
03         margin: 5px 0;
04         line-height: 1;     }
05  ul li {
06         list-style: none;
07         list-style-position: inside;
08         background: transparent url(../_images/
                flourish-left.png) no-repeat 0 center;
09         padding: 25px;       }
```

Nulla sed felis. Sed et tellus. Vivamus venenatis suscipit magna. Vestibulum hendrerit iaculis nunc. Morbi posuere tempus elit.

Ut commodo mattis nisi. Vestibulum tortor.Vivamus elit.

Nam nisi felis, egestas et, varius in, suscipit at, risus. Lorem ipsum dolor sit amet, consectetur adipiscing elit. Sed eget sapien.

Suspendisse aliquam suscipit elit. Sed a lorem. Suspendisse fermentum dolor in nibh dignissim bibendum.

Etiam a eros et odio dapibus tempus. Phasellus ligula. Donec venenatis hendrerit tellus.

Vestibulum dapibus augue at augue. Nulla imperdiet. Maecenas sed erat id neque lobortis elementum. Proin eleifend magna ac turpis. Curabitur magna sapien, convallis vitae, imperdiet non, sagittis aliquam, tellus. Nunc pretium orci cursus nisl facilisis pulvinar.

RIJKSMUSEUM

↖ Home

Collection

- The Masterpieces
- Preview paintings catalogue
- Rijksmuseum widget
- Explore 1000 Major exhibits
- Webspecials
- Search the collection
- Art Collection
- History Collection
- Collection Drawings, Prints & Photographs
- Acquisitions
- Works of art - FAQ
- Photoservice

Enter searchphrase →

all

Search the collection

Read more →

Collection

◀ Read this page

THE MASTERPIECES ↘

The Masterpieces
While the restoration of the main building is underway, the Rijksmuseum is displaying the crème de la crème of its permanent collection in the newly furnished Philips Wing. 'Rijksmuseum, The Masterpieces' offers the unique opportunity to view all the highlights of the Golden Age in one place.

↘ Read more

1000 MAJOR EXHIBITS ↘

Explore 1000 major exhibits

↘ Read more

RIJKSMUSEUM WIDGET ↘

Masterpiece on your desktop
New version! Place the widget on your site or weblog.

↘ Read more

SEARCH THE COLLECTION ↘

Search the collection

↘ Read more

ACQUISITIONS ↘

Dioramas from Surinam

↘ Read more

ART COLLECTION ↘

Paintings, Sculpture, Applied Art and Asiatic Art

↘ Read more

COLLECTION HISTORY ↘

Authentic sources from the past

↘ Read more

THE PRINTROOM ↘

Drawings, Prints & Photographs

↘ Read more

FAQ ↘

How can I find information on a particular artist?

↘ Read more

◉ CHOOSE ANOTHER LANGUAGE
✉ KEEP ME INFORMED
✆ CONTACT

Enter searchphrase

SEARCH

all

Webspecials

↘ **The Masterpieces**

REMBRANDT CARAVAGGIO
↘ **Rembrandt - Caravaggio**

JAN VAN DER HEYDEN
2 FEBRUARY - 20 APRIL
↘ **Fire!**

Related links

↘ All the webspecials

E-tickets →

Why queue for tickets, when you can buy them online?

E-mail newsletter →

All the latest about activities at the museum and other related information.

Webshop →

Books, reproductions and lots more.

Hypertext links allow you to jump around a Web page, a Web site, or the entire Web. All links, whether internal or external, are created using the anchor tag (*<a>*) to link an image or text to another location. However, different types of links should be styled differently.

Hypertext links in a block of text generally have a different emphasis than site navigation, while buttons are used to highlight specific functionality. CSS provides us with an easy way to take a single HTML tag and give it a multitude of looks based on its context.

CHAPTER 10

NAVIGATION

CSS Sprites

All navigation in a Web browser, whether a hypertext link or a menu option, relies on the anchor tag (*a*). This tag has four distinct states accessed through the link pseudo-classes: *a:link*, *a:visited*, *a:hover*, and *a:active*. An effective way of showing the change in states is swapping the background image. However, image swapping has two important shortcomings:

01 **Download time** ⸻ Each image requires a separate file download, and the more files downloaded the longer your page takes to display.

02 **Image flashing** ⸻ Images are downloaded as needed, so the link images associated are not downloaded until the user interacts with the page. This can cause a delay the first time the image is needed.

To overcome these problems, developers use a technique called CSS sprites, placing all four link state images into a single image file and then using background positioning to move the background around within the text box boundaries. The unneeded images are waiting and ready but cropped from view by the elements text box.

Rijksmuseum
www.rijksmuseum.nl

The Web site for the Dutch Rijksmuseum uses an innovative combination of navigation techniques, including horizontal and vertical menus.

background: transparent
  url(../_images/icon-pointer-sprite.png)
  no-repeat right 0;
height: 15px;
_height: 20px;
padding: 0 40px 5px 0;

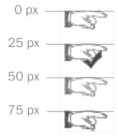

icon-pointer-sprite.png

Link

background-position: right 0;

Visited

background-position: right -25px;

Hover

background-position: right -50px;

Active

background-position: right -75px;

Links

Remember to style links not only for how they will appear when the page first loads, but also for the different states they have as the user interacts with them. You should style each of the four link states separately. In addition, since all links are controlled through the same HTML tag, it's important to differentiate their styles based on context.

For voxLibris, a default style has been set up to turn underlining off in all four states and then to set a color for all four of the states (01–08). You can set other styles, of course, but color is the most common way to differentiate link states.

Should Links Be Underlined?

Traditionally, hypertext links have been underlined to help them stand out. Underlining is a typographically unattractive way of highlighting links, however, in part because the line color is the same as the text color, creating visual clutter.

There are many alternatives to using the underline style for links, such as using a background color or image, as shown in voxLibris.

If you do want links underlined, a better alternative to the underline style is to use a *border-bottom* property. This creates an effect similar to underlining the link, but you can control the color, thickness, and style of the line, allowing for a more sublime design.

If the link is in a paragraph, styles are also included to add a background image—one that mimics a highlight marker—that differentiates these links from others, such as those in the navigation menu and genre list (12–15).

Links can also be given the class *readmore* within a paragraph to be given special treatment using CSS sprites as described in the previous section (16–28).

```
01  /*-------------------------------------------------
02      Links - Defaults
03  -------------------------------------------------*/
04  a            {      text-decoration: none;      }
05  a:link       {      color: rgb(0,85,126);       }
06  a:visited    {      color: rgb(0,50,75);        }
07  a:hover      {      color: rgb(0,170,255);      }
08  a:active     {      color: rgb(255,215,0);      }
```

voxLIBRIS provides public domain audiobooks you can download free of charge.

Genres
About
News
Reviews
Donate
Contact

```
09  /*-------------------------------------------------
10      Links - Paragraph
11  -------------------------------------------------*/
12  p a:link, p a:visited {
13      background: transparent
            url(../_images/bg-p-a-link.png)
            repeat-x 0 -2px;  }
14  p a:hover    {
            background-position: -20px -2px;    }
15  p a:active    {    background-image: none; }
16  p a.readmore {
17      position: relative;
18      background: transparent
            url(../_images/icon-pointer-sprite.png)
            no-repeat right 0;
19      padding: 0 40px 5px 0;
20      _background: none;       }
21  p a.readmore:link {
22      background-position: right 0;     }
23  p a.readmore:visited {
24      background-position: right -25px;    }
25  p a.readmore:hover {
26      background-position: right -50px;    }
27  p a.readmore:active {
28      background-position: right -75px;    }
```

New Categories Coming Next Month

Lorem ipsum dolor sit amet, consectetur adipiscing elit. Vestibulum commodo metus sit amet libero. Cras nisl neque, lacinia id, mollis vel, dictum ac, ante. Vestibulum tortor. **Lorem ipsum dolor sit amet.**

Read More ☞

Menus

Menus are a list of links that allow the user to navigate sections and sub-sections within a Web site. Although the links could simply be grouped together, it's better to use the list tag (*<li>*) to show their relationship. Navigation links also use the anchor tag, but some different styles should be added to differentiate them. Whether the top level (sometimes called "global") navigation menus run horizontally or vertically, it's imperative that they are clear and easy to identify.

- **Horizontal menus** generally run down the left column of the page, providing top level navigation for the Web site (29–36).

- **Vertical menus** built from a list of links are floated next to each other, generally somewhere at the top of the page above or below the header. Vertical menus also tend to be placed on the footer ostensibly as backup navigation, but actually because it improves search engine optimization (37–46).

```
29   /*------------------------------------------------
30         Menus
31   ------------------------------------------------*/
32   #menumain ul.menu li {
33        display: block;
34        padding: 5px 0;
35        border-top: 1px solid rgb(192,192,192);
36        width: 100%; }
```

GENRES
ABOUT
NEWS
REVIEWS
DONATE
CONTACT

```
37   /*------------------------------------------------
38         Menu - Footer
39   ------------------------------------------------*/
40   #footer ul.menu li {
41        float: left;
42        padding: 3px 20px;
43        margin: 0;
44        background: none;
45        border-left: 1px solid rgb(128,128,128);       }
46   #footer ul.menu li a:link,#footer ul.menu li a:visited {
          color: rgb(105,105,105);         }
```

| GENRES | ABOUT | NEWS | REVIEWS | DONATE | CONTACT |

UXBooth

uxbooth.com

UXBooth—a Web site that offers free usability reviews and articles about user experience on the Web—uses a horizontal menu placed clearly across the top of the page.

"blink" is it morning already? ugh.

i think today there will be coffee brewed. mmmmm hot goodnesss....

love
hate
think
believe
feel
wish

i think I shall find "Solace" in a dark cool theater this morning. :)

i think I'll make chicken noodle soup in the crock pot for dinner. Jamie will appreciate it and it's one of Cassie's favorites. Plus easy!

Welcoming minymouse to the following. Great to have you on board.

i think I know who you are, but I'm not sure. Time will tell.

Or so

i think? Today was canceled and I slept all afternoon. GLORIOUS!!!

I dont know why but

i think this fog is beautiful!

twistori
this is the first step in an ongoing social experiment, based on twitter. inspired by wefeelfine. hand-crafted by amy hoy and thomas fuchs. get the mac os x screensaver.

Twistori

twistori.com

Twistori scrolls a feed of Tweets that include the keywords love, hate, think, believe, feel, and wish. You can switch between keywords using the vertical menu.

Buttons

Buttons are used to highlight important content on a site that may not fit into a global menu.

voxLibris has buttons for each of the genres it covers (50–68 and 95–118). Rather than simply placing an image tag in the HTML—which limits future design possibilities—each button has an ID associated with it to load a specific background image, which is placed into the list tag with some design enhancements using *border-radius* and *box-shadow*. The final trick is to move the caption text underneath the button image by setting the top margin in the list tag to 50px.

On top of this (literally), in the anchor tag, a transparent PNG background is used to create a gel effect, so that the button looks like it has a glossy top (69–91). To avoid trouble, I'm turning this off in IE6 with *_background: none;*.

button-gel-100.png

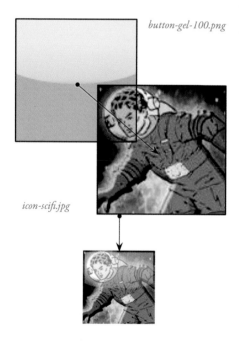

icon-scifi.jpg

```
47   /*------------------------------------------------------------
48          Article 1 - Genre List
49   ------------------------------------------------------------*/
50   #genrelist .genrelistbuttons { list-style: none;     }
51   #genrelist .genrelistbuttons li {
52          background: none;
53          height: auto;
54          padding: 0;
55          font-size: .875em;
56          float: left;
57          text-align: center;
58          background: rgb(105,105,105)
                 url(../_images/genreicons/icon-adventure.jpg)
                 no-repeat center center;
59          display: block;
60          width: 100px;
61          height: 100px;
62          margin: 15px 15px 50px 0;
63          -webkit-border-radius: 10px;
64          -moz-border-radius: 10px;
65          border-radius: 10px;
66          -webkit-box-shadow: rgb(0,0,0) 0 0 5px;
67          -moz-box-shadow: rgb(0,0,0) 0 0 5px;
68          box-shadow: rgb(0,0,0) 0 0 5px;        }
69   #genrelist .genrelistbuttons li a {
70          display: block;
71          opacity: 1;
72          width: 100%;
73          background: transparent
                 url(../_images/button-gel-100.png)
                 no-repeat 0 0;
74          _background: none;
75          padding-top: 105px;
76          color: rgb(169,169,169);
77          -webkit-border-radius: 10px;
78          -moz-border-radius: 10px;
79          border-radius: 10px;        }
80   #genrelist .genrelistbuttons li a em {
81          display: block;
82          margin-bottom: 5px;
83          font-style: normal;
84          line-height: 1;
85          font-size: 1.25em;
86          color: rgb(105,105,105);
87          font-family:
                 garamond, cochin, cambria, times, serif;     }
88   #genrelist .genrelistbuttons li a:hover {
89          opacity: .6;
90          border-color: rgb(0,170,255);
91          color: rgb(0,0,0);     }
```

```
92    /*------------------------------------------------------------
93           Article 1 - Genre List - Icons
94    ------------------------------------------------------------*/
95    #genrelist .genrelistbuttons li.genre-adventure {
96           background-image: url(../_images/genreicons/
                  icon-adventure.jpg);     }
97    #genrelist .genrelistbuttons li.genre-anthropology {
98           background-image: url(../_images/genreicons/
                  icon-anthropology.jpg);  }
99    #genrelist .genrelistbuttons li.genre-children {
100          background-image: url(../_images/genreicons/
                  icon-children.jpg);      }
101   #genrelist .genrelistbuttons li.genre-epic {
102          background-image: url(../_images/genreicons/
                  icon-epic.jpg);     }
103   #genrelist .genrelistbuttons li.genre-fantasy {
104          background-image: url(../_images/genreicons/
                  icon-fantasy.jpg);  }
105   #genrelist .genrelistbuttons li.genre-history {
106          background-image: url(../_images/genreicons/
                  icon-history.jpg);  }
107   #genrelist .genrelistbuttons li.genre-humor {
108          background-image: url(../_images/genreicons/
                  icon-humor.jpg);    }
109   #genrelist .genrelistbuttons li.genre-medical {
110          background-image: url(../_images/genreicons/
                  icon-medical.jpg);  }
111   #genrelist .genrelistbuttons li.genre-mystery {
112          background-image: url(../_images/genreicons/
                  icon-mystery.jpg);  }
113   #genrelist .genrelistbuttons li.genre-philosophy {
114          background-image: url(../_images/genreicons/
                  icon-philosophy.jpg);    }
115   #genrelist .genrelistbuttons li.genre-romance {
116          background-image: url(../_images/genreicons/
                  icon-romance.jpg);     }
117   #genrelist .genrelistbuttons li.genre-scifi {
118          background-image: url(../_images/genreicons/
                  icon-scifi.jpg);     }
```

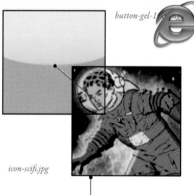

Using Design Enhancements

Just because a browser does not support a particular property does not mean you shouldn't use it—as long as it does not interfere with the other browsers.

For example, in the three cases here, the buttons are displayed and easily accessible. FF3, which supports *border-radius*, has rounded corners, Sa4, which supports both *box-shadow* and *border-radius* has rounded corners and a drop shadow. Compare these two versions to IE8, which does not support either of the properties. The buttons are still just as usable, but not quite as slick looking.

You could use images to create the same look and feel in all three browsers, but CSS design enhancements provide several advantages:

Easy to change—Design changes can be made directly in the CSS without having to recut images.

Design flexibility—Design elements like drop shadows and rounded corners are difficult to achieve with images.

Smaller files sizes—CSS code will generally download faster than an image file.

Future compatibility—All of these styles will be standard on all browsers in the future, but the kludge you used to get an image solution to work now may not work later.

CSS3.info

css3.info

Learn about the latest advances in CSS Level 3 with a designer's perspective. At CSS3.info, you can get a designer's perspective on the latest advances in CSS Level 3. It takes the W3C jargon and makes it comprehensible.

The chrome (or "skin") of a Web page is made up of the visual elements that give it its look and feel. Using backgrounds, you can add visual elements to your page to frame and highlight the content of your Web page and guide the user's eye around.

Although images are often thought to be embedded directly into the page using the *<img>* tag, this severely limits the versatility of your designs by hard coding the images into the structure. Instead, most Web designs place all graphic interface element on the page using the CSS background property, and reserve the HTML image tag strictly for content such as photos, illustrations, and figures.

CHAPTER 11

CHROME

Using Transparent Images

The PNG image format is now standard on all Web browsers, allowing you to include an alpha channel in images. You can have areas in your image with an opacity anywhere between 0% and 100%. Rounded corners, drop shadows, or any non-rectangular shapes (such as text) can be used against any background. This differs from GIF transparency where the pixels are either visible or not.

Create PNG images using most standard image editing software (such as Photoshop or Fireworks). There are three different PNG formats, varying in image quality and file size:

- **PNG-8**: Works a lot like the GIF format, indexing all of the colors in the image down to a maximum of 256. Support: Fireworks and Photoshop, although Photoshop does not include the alpha channel indexed transparency, where a color is either visible or 100% transparent.

- **PNG-24**: Works like JPEG, producing higher quality images with color shifts. However, for images like photographs, PNG-24 tends to create larger images than JPEG. Support: Photoshop and Fireworks, although Fireworks does not support the alpha channel.

- **PNG-32**: An even higher-quality image format than PNG-24, but it creates larger files. Support: Fireworks.

ColourLovers

colourlovers.com

Looking for colorful inspiration? Check out ColourLovers, a design community centered around following color trends.

Transparent **PNG**

Transparent **GIF**

Using Transparent Images *continued*

Fixing Transparent PNGs in IE6

To learn more about the underscore hack see Appendix C, "Fixing Internet Explorer."

The downside to transparent PNGs is IE6. Although it displays PNG images, it does not automatically display them as transparent. Instead, you have to disable the background property and then use a special filter to load the image.

For example, to use the voxLibris logo on a gradient background, save it on a transparent PNG, and use it as a background image:

background: transparent url(../_images/logo-voxlibris.png) no-repeat 0 0;

In IE6, this will appear with a gray background where the image should be transparent. Now add the following code immediately underneath in the CSS rule:

_background: none;

_filter: progid:DXImageTransform. Microsoft.AlphaImageLoader (src="../_images/logo-voxlibris.png", sizingMethod="crop");

Fixing The Fix

Use this trick sparingly. There are some problems with links and form fields if they are on any part of the transparent area of a PNG image; they simply will not work. To fix this problem, you need to set positioning for that link or form element: *a { position: relative; }.*

Using the AlphaImageLoader can also slow down the page loading in IE6. An alternative is to always use PNG-8 images for the background and no AlphaImageLoader, but these will not look quite as good in IE6.

Now the transparent PNG will appear as expected using the AlphaImageLoader and the underscore hack to hide this from other browsers. You have two options for the sizing method: *crop* and *scale*. *Crop* will show the image once, while *scale* stretches the image to fill the area. You cannot tile backgrounds with the AlphaImageLoader.

background: transparent url(../_images/logo-voxlibris.png) no-repeat 0 0;

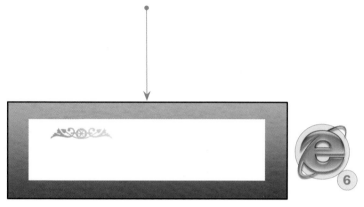

_background: none;

_filter: progid:DXImageTransform.Microsoft.AlphaImageLoader (src="../_images/logo-voxlibris.png", sizingMethod="crop");

Defining the Grid

bg-body.png

Although the grid of columns and rows is created in the layout, it is often visually defined using background colors and images. This includes a background for the body of the document and then different backgrounds to separate the different grid elements.

Columns

bg-page.png

Designers often prefer balanced columns—that is, columns that appear to be the same height. One of the drawbacks of layout with CSS is that you cannot bind column heights together, so, invariably, one column will be shorter than the others.

A common workaround for this problem is to visually define columns using a background image placed in the page element, which is the parent element to all of the column, and will thus stretch the height of the tallest column in it as long as you remember to put the *<br style="alignclear" />* before the closing *</div>* tag as described in Chapter 8.

For voxLibris, the right column (*#aside2*) is visually defined by a dark cloth pattern in the page element background (*#page*), different from the speckled paper pattern of the larger left side, which includes both the left column (*#aside1*) and center column (*#article1*).

```
01    /*--------------------------------------------------------------

02         Chrome - Grid

03    --------------------------------------------------------------*/

04    body { background: rgb(0,50,75)
             url(../_images/bg-body.png) repeat 0 0;        }

05    #page {

06         background: transparent
              url(../_images/bg-page.png) repeat-y 0 0;

07         padding: 0 16px;

08         _background: none;

09         _filter: progid:DXImageTransform.Microsoft.AlphaImageLoader
             (src="../_images/bg-page.png", sizingMethod="scale"); }
```

Defining the Grid *continued*

Rows

bg-header.png

Rows stretch horizontally across the area defined across the page area and can be visually defined with a solid color background color or background image. If you use a gradient, then you may want to have it only repeat horizontally (*repeat-x*) so that the gradient doesn't create a repeating pattern, but make sure to set the bottom color in your gradient as the background color for the row so that there is a smooth color transition.

The voxLibris header and footer use the same repeating gradient image (*bg-header.png*) as the background. I opted to reuse the same image in both. Different images could have been used, but since they have the same appearance, this reduces the number of images that have to be downloaded, thus speeding up the page display.

10   *#header, #footer { background: transparent*
                url(../_images/bg-header.png) repeat-x 0 0; }
11   *#footer {   background-position: 0 bottom; }*

Logos and Forms

Logos

logo-voxlibris.png

Text replacement is any process where HTML is replaced by an image. There are several ways to achieve text replacement, but the best is to use the text in a background image, in an element that includes the text in the HTML.

Begin by specifying the width and height of the element that will contain your graphic text. Set the background image source to the image with the text. Then set the line height to three times the height of the element and set overflow to hidden, so all text is pushed out of the box and will not be displayed.

The voxLibris logo uses the Fontin Sans font, which is not a standard font, so we'll need to put it into a graphic. We'll use the level 1 header tag in the *#header* to create the logo, including the text "voxLibris". Set the *width* and *height* to be the same as the image and then triple the line height.

Forms

bg-grad01.png

Form elements are often overlooked as an important element to skin. Most browsers have a default style for form elements that is, to be polite, hideously ugly, especially if the rest of the site is well designed.

For voxLibris, simple gradient, border, and font size changes are all that are needed to spruce up the form fields.

```
12    /*-------------------------------------------------
13              Chrome - Header - voxLIBRIS logo
14    -------------------------------------------------*/
15    #header h1 {
16        position: absolute;
17        left: 0;
18        bottom: -2px;
19        width: 306px;
20        height: 66px;
21        line-height: 188px;
22        overflow: hidden;
23        background: transparent
             url(../_images/logo-voxlibris.png)
             no-repeat 0 0;
24        _background: none;
25        _filter: progid:DXImageTransform.Microsoft.
             AlphaImageLoader(src='../_images/logo-
             voxlibris.png', sizingMethod='crop');}
```

```
26    /*-------------------------------------------------
27              Chrome - Header - Search
28    -------------------------------------------------*/
29    #header .search input, #header .search select {
30        background: transparent
             url(../_images/bg-grad01.png) repeat-x
             center center;
31        border: 1px solid rgb(102,102,102);
32        height: 25px;
33        width: 200px;
34        font-size: 1.2em;
35        padding: 0 10px;
36        margin-bottom: 5px;
37        -moz-border-radius: 5px;
38        -webkit-border-radius: 5px;
39        border-radius: 5px;}
40    #header .search select {
41        background-image:
             url(../_images/bg-grad01.png);
42        padding-right: 0;   }
```

Defining Sections

Sections and modules will often have specialized backgrounds to set them off from surrounding content. The module will have a header and footer to cap a central content area whose height will stretch as needed.

bg-sidebar1-head.png
bg-sidebar1-mid.png
bg-sidebar1-foot.png

- **Footer**: The background cap for the module is set in the background for the entire module, with its position set to bottom.

- **Header**: The header cap image is added to a level 2 header tag, with no repeating. This also means that the amount of content for the header text is limited to the height of the background image.

- **Content**: A special class is added around the content of the module and a background repeated vertically behind that.

Since transparent PNGs are used for all three backgrounds, the background color is set to transparent.

Alternate Version for Ads

You can also create variations on this module, as is the case with the voxLibris's ad module, simply by changing the background image source.

bg-ad-head.png
bg-ad-mid.png
bg-ad-foot.png

```
43    /*-------------------------------------------------
44          Chrome - Aside 1 - Section
45    -------------------------------------------------*/
46    #aside1 .section {
47          background: transparent
                url(../_images/bg-sidebar1-foot.png)
                no-repeat 0 bottom;          }
48    #aside1 .section h2 {
49          background: transparent
                url(../_images/bg-sidebar1-head.png)
                no-repeat 0 0;
50          text-align: left;
51          max-height: 136px;
52          overflow: hidden;
53          font-variant: small-caps;
54          color: red;     }
55    #aside1 .section div.content {
56          background: transparent
                url(../_images/bg-sidebar1-mid.png) repeat-y
                0 0; }
57    #aside1 .section p, #aside1 .section ul {
58          list-style-position: inside;
59          list-style-type: none;}
60    /*-------------------------------------------------
61          Chrome - Aside 1 - Ads
62    -------------------------------------------------*/
63    #aside1 .ads {
64          background-image:
                url(../_images/bg-ads-foot.png);       }
65
66    #aside1 .ads h2 {
67          background-image:
                url(../_images/bg-ads-head.png);       }
68
69    #aside1 .ads div.content {
70          background-image:
                url(../_images/bg-ads-mid.png);        }
71
72    #aside1 .ads p {
73          color: rgb(0,0,0);
74          padding: 10px 80px;       }
```

WELCOME

voxLIBRIS provides public domain
audiobooks you can download free of
charge.

GENRES

ABOUT

NEWS

REVIEWS

DONATE

CONTACT

Top 50 WTF Comic Moments
Countdown The Most Outrageous
Moments In Comic Book History!
www.UCO.com/Comics

HP Global Citizenship
Why Protecting Privacy is Essential For
Socially Responsible Companies
www.hp.com

Environments
Find Environments & More
Environments Options Here!
Octopedia.com

Ads by Oogle

Adventure
34 books

Fantasy
13 books

Mystery
67 books

About

Nulla sed feli[
iaculis nunc.
Vestibulum t[
Lorem ipsum

Suspendisse a
dignissim bib
ligula. Donec
imperdiet. M[
eleifend magr[
sagittis aliqua[

Read More

News

voxLIBR[
New Bo[

Lorem ipsum
consectetur a[
commodo me[
nisl neque, la[
ac, ante. Vest[

Defining Sections *continued*

Final Flourishes

flourish-up.png

flourish-down.png

Another way to define sections on the page is to add rules and flourishes that guide the visitor's eye to important locations. Flourishes can take a number of forms but should fit with the general appearance of your design.

The flourishes in the voxLibris article1 section are similar to those in the logo and in other areas throughout the page. They are added in the backgrounds of the section and the headlines to give a top and bottom treatment.

Should I Use a Class or an ID?

In Chapter 4, I discussed the difference between a class and an ID—an ID is used to identify a specific element on the screen for specific placement or for control by JavaScript. Still, it can be tough sometimes to determine which elements should use an ID and which should use a class.

If you will be reusing a style *or are likely to reuse a style*, use a class. For example, in voxLibris, *#article1* is an ID because it is being used to define the central content element, and will only ever appear once on a page. However, *.ads* is a class even though there is only one element tagged with ads. It's possible that there may be multiple ad blocks included on a page, even if there are not on this page.

```
75    /*----------------------------------------------------------------
76          Chrome - Article
77    ----------------------------------------------------------------*/
78    #article1 .section h1 {
79          padding-top: 30px;
80          text-transform: uppercase;
81          text-align: center;
82          background: transparent
                url(../_images/flourish-up.png) no-repeat
                center top;
83          _background: none;        }
84    #article1 .section {
85          background-position: bottom center;
86          padding-bottom: 50px;
87          margin-bottom: 3px;
88          background: transparent
                url(../_images/flourish-up.png) no-repeat
                center bottom;
89          _background: none;}
90    #article1 .section h2 {
91          font-variant: small-caps;
92          margin: 3px 0 30px 0;
93          height: 35px;
94          background: transparent
                url(../_images/flourish-down.png) no-repeat
                center 3px;
95          border-top: 1px solid rgb(128,128,128);
96          _background: none;        }
97    #article1 .section h3 {
98          font-family: "fontin sans", optima, candara,
                "trebuchet-MS", sans-serif;
99          height: 50px;
100         margin-top: 20px;  }
101   #article1 .section p {
102         margin-bottom: 20px;      }
103   #article1 ul li {
104         list-style: none;
105         list-style-position: inside;
106         background: transparent
                url(../_images/flourish-left.png) no-repeat 0
                center;
107         padding: 10px 25px;
108         _background: none;        }
```

GOOD

$857,220 raised

0 —————→ $1M

Learn more

| Blogs | Magazine | Video | Events | Community |

SEARCH

Video: GOOD News

NOV. 14, 2008

Casual Friday

GOOD News: Deconstructing Bond
Numbers and Holloway discuss 007. More

Blog

A New Day for Exoskeletons
How a previously lost idea for superhuman strength found its way.

Read more...

Blog

GOOD Sheet: You Want to Help
GOOD and Piece Studio look at national service.

Read more...

Blog

350 or Bust!
Ben Jervey on the most important number in the world.

Read more...

Video

Part 5: Legs With Brains
Robotics and the next generation of prosthetics.

Read more...

◀ ▶

Saturday, November 15, 2008

2 ⚙

This Week in GOOD

Posted by: **Patrick James** on November 14, 2008 at 7:40 pm

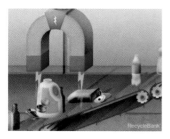

Do you ever wonder what happens to your plastic, paper, or what have you after you toss it into the recycling bin? If so, then you are in luck. Our chums over at Recycle Bank (we've talked about them before) have created an interactive piece that walks you through each stage of the, um, cycle. Watch and learn.

This week wasn't all fun and games. It began on a sad note with the passing of Miriam...

Read & Discuss ▶▶▶

Filed under: **Blog** : *Good Blog* | Categories: **Magazine**

✎ Share ▼   💬 Discuss   ⚙ GOODmark ?

---

1 💬

Breathing Room

Posted by: **Andrew Price** on November 14, 2008 at 7:39 pm

In what is being touted as "a major step in bringing about a clean energy economy," a new coal plant in Utah was told it had to mitigate its carbon dioxide emissions with the "best available control technology."

In the case, the Environmental Appeals Board, an independent court within the Environmental Protection Agency, ruled against the EPA itself, which has tried to weasel out of regulating carbon dioxide for years.

From *TIME*:

"The board's decision will force the EPA...

Read & Discuss ▶▶▶

seventh GENERATION

Tampons
Tampons made with non-organic cotton can expose you and the environment to harmful pesticides. Find out if your personal products contain pesticides with the Label Reading Guide.

Learn More ▶   Spin Again ▶

Advertisement

RECENT CONTRIBUTORS

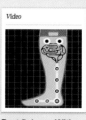

💬 MOST DISCUSSED

1. The 51 Best* Magazines Ever
2. Stop Teaching Handwriting
3. Design 21 Contest Giveaway
4. Playing Doctor
5. Unconscious Consumption
6. The New Nostradamus
7. The Mormons Are Coming!
8. It's Time to Flee the Country
9. God, Without the Fuss
10. Cold Turkey

That's about it. If you've read this book front to back, you should now understand the fundamentals of CSS—how to speak it and how to understand it. Like any language, there is always more to learn—nuances that turns humdrum prose into compelling poetry.

In this last chapter, I want to offer a few parting words about the state of CSS and to review some of the best practices I've stressed throughout the book.

CHAPTER 12

THE LAST WORD

CSS Validation

I've mentioned throughout this book that CSS is a standard created by the World Wide Web Consortium (W3C), and that the browser manufacturers then interpret this standard—with varying degrees of success—to create their products. In theory, since there is an accepted standard CSS, there is "perfect" CSS code that exactly follows these standards.

The W3C has created a Web site that will validate your CSS code, checking that it adheres to the W3C specified CSS standard. To use the W3C Validation Service:

01 Visit *jigsaw.w3.org/css-validator/*.

02 Enter a URL, upload a file, or enter your CSS directly.

03 Click the Check button.

04 Hold your breath while waiting to see whether or not your code is valid. Any errors in your code will be highlighted by line number, showing the exact problem.

If there are problems, don't sweat it. First check what the errors are. Some of the "hacks" we use to create Web sites that work cross-browser will cause errors, even though they do not interfere with the page displaying.

Good

good.is

Good is an online and print-based magazine devoted to people who "give a damn."

Designing for Web Standards?

Standards are important. The closer we can get to ideal CSS, the better it is for everybody. If we could simply code to the CSS standard and know our designs would display the same way in all browsers, what a wonderful world it would be.

That's not the world we live in.

In our world, we have to deal with multiple browsers that conflict with each other. Writing code that meets the strict W3C standards is all fine and good, but completely unrealistic if you expect your code to actually work. The fact is most CSS code on the Web will not validate, because working designers have to be more concerned with making their Web pages look right across multiple browsers than with meeting some perfect code ideal. Many of the techniques I've shown you for getting your code to work cross-browser, such as the underscore hack to get IE6 to play nice with widths and padding, will not validate.

I recommend validating your CSS code as a last step in the QA process, to help you find any true errors in your code that you need to fix. But look closely at the errors raised. Make sure it is not simply flagging code you are using to get your designs to work cross-browser.

It is far more important that your code works, is fast, and is easy to edit than it is for it to be valid according to the W3C.

HTML Validation

Although "errors" in your CSS can be acceptable if you need to include code for IE6, errors in your HTML can be the cause of many browser "quirks" that will cause problems with your designs.

Validate your HTML code at *validator.w3.org*.

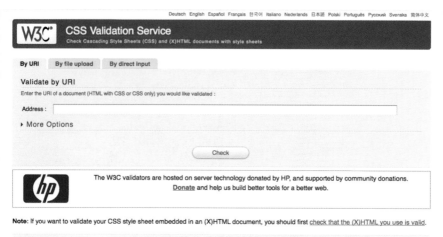

W3C CSS Validation Service

jigsaw.w3.org/css-validator

Provided free of charge, the CSS Validation Service will prowl through your code to find deviations from the CSS standards. But beware: It will show errors if you use common tricks like the underscore hack or design enhancements like *-webkit-box-shadow*, so take the results with a grain of salt.

CSS Import

cssimport.com

If you are looking for a well-designed site, check out CSS Import, which highlights the best CSS design from around the Web. Don't expect any of these sites to pass muster with the strict W3C CSS Validation Service.

CSS Frameworks

A CSS framework is a library of generic styles that can be easily applied to most Web designs. They come in the form of pre-built external style sheets that package ready-made design solutions for common elements such as headers, columns, footers, and sections. Using a CSS framework allows designers quick and easy access to well tested, cross-browser compatible, and standards-compliant CSS code. This tends to speed development of better code.

On the downside, when you use a CSS framework you import code that you may or may not use, but which will increase download time. In addition, you are relying on pre-built code that might limit your design choices. There are a wide variety of CSS frameworks, so choosing one will depend on what you need it to do.

Here are some popular CSS frameworks to get you started:

Blueprint ⟿ Provides a solid layout grid, typographic controls, and a style sheet for printing. LINK: *blueprintcss.org*

Emastic ⟿ Uses ems to create elastic layouts.
LINK: *code.google.com/p/emastic*

Typogridphy ⟿ Uses 12- and 16-column grids at 960px wide and typographic style rules for "creating vertical rhythm."
LINK: *csswizardry.com/typogridphy/*

YAML ⟿ "Yet Another Multicolumn Layout" provides flexible multi-column layouts that are easy to edit and modify.
LINK: *yaml.de*

YUI Grids ⟿ Yahoo's CSS Grids framework provides fixed and fluid layouts. LINK: *developer.yahoo.com/yui/grids*

Creating Your Own CSS Frameworks

If you are working in an environment where multiple sources are creating your Web content, you need a common library of styles. To facilitate a consistent layout, you can create your own CSS framework, often simple editorial styles, that the group then shares and can apply to their content. This also helps prevent writers or editors from adding inline or embedded styles when they need a particular style.

Beyond standard CSS best practices, there are a few things to keep in mind when creating your own CSS framework:

- **Use a class name prefix to ensure that your framework will not conflict with other classes.**
  Add a three- to six-letter prefix before all framework classes to ensure they do not conflict with other styles.

- **Keep the rules as generic as possible.**
  These styles should provide bare-bones styling so as not to interfere with other site-wide styles.

- **Provide styles for common layout elements such as columns, drop-boxes, article excerpts, small print, and image captions.**
  Framework styles should be used primarily for layout and for creating commonly used editorial styles.

CSS for Other Media

Mobile Devices

Setting the media type is explained in the "Media" section of Chapter 5, "Semantics."

Mobile devices are a popular way to access the Web, but not particularly good for displaying Web pages designed for larger screens. Fortunately, CSS allows you to set style sheets specifically for mobile screens, but you need to keep a few things in mind when creating mobile designs:

- **Use a single column with no horizontal scrolling.**
  Most mobile devices have a portrait rather than landscape orientation, which limits horizontal design.

- **Provide constant top level navigation and hide secondary navigation.**
  Many mobile devices have little or no built-in browser navigation, so the designer needs to include back buttons as well as top level navigation. You do not need a complete index of the site, though, since mobile devices often require the user to navigate through all links in order to select one of them.

- **Minimize the use of foreground and background images.**
  Although images might be a necessary part of the content, it's better to provide links to larger images and eliminate any background images altogether. This makes pages faster to load and easier to read on small screens.

- **Keep the design simple.**
  Simple, well-structured pages will be much easier to use on small mobile screens.

Print

Viewing a printed Web page is a very different experience than viewing it on a screen (even a small screen). Paper, by its very nature, is not hyper-textual. However, paper is more portable and cheaper than a computer, and many of your visitors will opt to print Web pages rather than reading them on the screen. To that end, you should adapt your designs for print:

- **Hide navigation and ads.**
  No matter how hard you press on the piece of paper, it will not jump to another piece of paper. So all linked elements should be hidden by using *display: none*.

- **Consider colors and images carefully.**
  Remember that what looks good on the screen doesn't necessarily look good when printed.

- **Do not rely on background images for layout or bullets.**
  Many people will turn background images off, so do not assume those images will print.

- **Use point sizes for font sizes.**
  Although not preferred for screen layout, point sizes are perfect for print.

- **Allow maximum width for important content.**
  Columns on printed pages should allow the maximum reading area for important content.

- **Display custom content such as link URLs and footers.**
  Since the reader may not have the URLs listed, set up your pages to list any link URLs either at the end of the article or next to the links in context.

CSS Best Practices

Throughout this book, I have attempted to present the vast range of techniques possible with CSS, knowing that the future of Web design with CSS is not in what we know how to do now, but in what we will learn to do in the future. That said, there are many well-tested techniques that are widely accepted as CSS best practices. Many of these best practices have more to do with the limitation of the medium and browsers than they do with good design practice, but knowing them can speed your development process and lead to better designs.

General

External style sheets are explained in "Where to Put Style Rules" in Chapter 5, "Semantics."

- **Use external style sheets.**
  The power of using CSS comes in its ability to make a single change that effects an entire Web site. This power is only possible, though, when styles are collected into external style sheet files.

- **Use *<link>* for speed and *@import* for flexibility.**
  @import has the advantage that it can be used equally well in both HTML documents and external CSS files. Unfortunately there are issues in IE—styles imported using *@import* will not load until after the content, causing a delay in page loading. If you notice problems with pages loading, use *<link>* instead of *@import*.

Screen, print, and handheld media are explained in "Media" in Chapter 5, "Semantics."

- **Link to CSS for screen, print, and handheld media.**
  CSS should be used to tailor the content for each output media. Designers need to consider how the page will look when printed or viewed on handheld devices.

Avoid inline styles.

Inline styles cannot be overridden, making it impossible to change whatever styles they set and limiting design flexibility. Inline styles also increase the code-to-text ratio, diminishing search engine optimization (SEO) and lowering your ranking in many search engines.

Avoid embedded styles in the body.

When placed in the body, embedded styles often render after the page content has loaded, causing an unattractive re-rendering of the page. They can also be difficult to override, difficult to find and edit, and can increase the code-to-text ratio, diminishing SEO.

If you have to use embedded styles, add them only in the *<head>* and keep them brief.

Although styles embedded in the *<head>* of the document will be rendered before the content is displayed, they limit design flexibility and will add more code, diminishing SEO.

Avoid !important.

Although a useful tool during development and prototyping of your site, making a declaration important reduces design flexibility and can often be confusing for later developers who may need to override the style.

!important is explained in "Importance" in Chapter 5, "Semantics."

Use concise, meaningful classes and IDs.

Avoid using names that describe the style being applied, as this will cause problems if those styles need to change. Instead, use names that describe the function of the class or ID. For example, instead of naming a class *redtext*, name it *hilight* or *hilighterror*.

CSS Best Practices *continued*

Design

- **Use *<img>* tags for image content (photos, illustrations, diagrams, and so on), not for your interface.**
  Placing an image in your HTML means that it cannot be easily styled or changed. Virtually all interface chrome— including icons, logos, controls, and buttons—can be added to the interface using background images in your CSS. This will cut down on the amount of code in your HTML, which is better for SEO, and allow for greater versatility when redesigning.

- **HTML should never be used for style, only for structure. HTML is intended to structure the page.**
  Placing tags such as *<b>* or *<i>* specify a particular style rather than structure. Instead use tags that add as few browser styles as possible, for example *<strong>* and *<em>*.

- **Avoid using padding and borders for fixed-dimension elements.**
  Problems with the IE6 implementation of the box model mean that padding and borders can be a hassle to deal with in any element with a fixed width and/or height. Try adding padding or margins to nested elements instead.

  For a quick fix to the box model problem, see "Fixing IE6" in Chapter 6, "Vocabulary."

- **Use CSS sprites for buttons and controls.**
  CSS sprites allow you to download fewer images and avoid the annoying "flash" as images load during link state changes.

  Use CSS sprites to add backgrounds to links, as described in Chapter 10, "Navigation" in the section "CSS Sprites."

Coding

- **Add comments to your CSS wherever possible to help explain what's going on.**
  Notes can be added as a last step in development, but should be included to help future designers and developers.

Comments are explained in the section "Adding Notes to CSS" in Chapter 5, "Semantics."

- **Always add a semicolon at the end of every declaration.**
  Even if it is the last CSS rule in the list, add the semicolon to avoid future aggravation.

- **Specify units except for 0.**
  0 is zero no matter what the unit, but in most cases a unit is needed. *line-height* and *opacity* are the two exceptions whose values do not have units.

For details about values in CSS, see Appendix B, "CSS Values."

- **Use RGB values for colors.**
  Although colors can be defined in a variety of ways in CSS, RGB values provide a broader gamut and are easier to change using JavaScript.

- **Use ems for all sizes *or* ems for font sizing, pixels for absolute sizes, and percentages for relative sizes.**
  There is an ongoing debate as to whether ems or pixels are better for creating Web designs. If you choose to go with all ems, you need to become familiar with a good pixel-to-em calculator, like Em Calculator (*riddle.pl/emcalc*).

- **Limit the scope of rules.**
  Using IDs and classes, you can ensure that styles are only applied where you want them and don't "leak" over into other areas or cause style conflicts.

CSS Best Practices *continued*

Optimizing

- **Use CSS property shortcuts wherever possible.**
  Many CSS properties can be combined into a single property using a shortcut. For example,
  border-top:5px; border-right:5px;
  border-bottom:1px; border-left:2px;
  can better be expressed as:
  border:5px 5px 1px 2px;

- **Don't add redundant styles.**
  Once a style property is set for an element, it will be inherited by all elements with that selector type (HTML, class, or ID) on the page and their child elements.

- **Use as few IDs as possible, and use each only once per Web page.**
  The more IDs you have, the more complicated your code gets. Generally you can get by with only a few IDs for major page grid sections. If you can use more than one ID in a contextual selector, you've got too many IDs.

- **Use as few classes as possible.**
  As with IDs, the more classes on your page, the more complicated your code. Classes are useful for styling similar types of elements, but not every instance of an element needs its own class.

- **Try to end contextual rules with an HTML selector.**
  Although not a hard and fast rule, the more CSS contextual rules you can end with an HTML selector, the more you are minimizing the number of IDs and classes in your code.

Appendixes

WELCOME

voxLIBRIS provides public domain audiobooks you can download free of charge.

GENRES

ABOUT

NEWS

REVIEWS

DONATE

CONTACT

Top 50 WTF Comic Moments
Countdown The Most Outrageous
Moments In Comic Book History!
www.UGO.com/Comics

HP Global Citizenship
Why Protecting Privacy is Essential
For Socially Responsible
Companies
www.hp.com

Environments
Find Environments & More
Environments Options Here!
Octopedia.com

Ads by Oogle

GENRES

Adventure
34 books

Anthropology
34 books

Children
34 books

Epic
34 books

Fantasy
34 books

History
34 books

Humor
34 books

Medical
34 books

Mystery
34 books

Philosophy
34 books

Romance
34 books

Science Fiction
34 books

ABOUT

Nulla sed felis. Sed et tellus. Vivamus venenatis suscipit magna. Vestibulum hendrerit iaculis nunc. Morbi posuere tempus elit. Ut commodo mattis nisi. **dictum ac, ante.** Vestibulum tortor.Vivamus elit. Nam nisi felis, egestas et, varius in, suscipit at, risus. Lorem ipsum dolor sit amet, consectuer adipiscing elit. Sed eget sapien.

Suspendisse aliquam suscipit elit. Sed a lorem. Suspendisse fermentum dolor in nibh dignissim bibendum. Etiam a eros et **dictum ac, ante** odio dapibus tempus. Phasellus ligula. Donec venenatis hendrerit tellus. Vestibulum dapibus augue at augue. Nulla imperdiet. Maecenas **dictum ac, ante** sed erat id neque lobortis elementum. Proin eleifend magna ac turpis. Curabitur magna sapien, convallis vitae, imperdiet non, sagittis aliquam, tellus. Nunc pretium orci cursus nisl facilisis pulvinar.

Read More

NEWS

voxLIBRIS Adds 30 New Books

Lorem ipsum dolor sit amet, **consectetur adipiscing elit.** Vestibulum commodo metus sit amet libero. Cras nisl neque, lacinia id, mollis vel, **dictum ac, ante.** Vestibulum tortor.

Read More

New Categories Coming Next Month

Lorem ipsum dolor sit amet, consectetur adipiscing elit. Vestibulum commodo metus sit amet libero. Cras nisl neque, lacinia id, mollis vel, dictum ac, ante. Vestibulum tortor. **Lorem ipsum dolor sit amet.**

Read More

REVIEWS

Bowolf by Unknown

Lorem ipsum dolor sit amet, **consectetur adipiscing elit.** Vestibulum commodo metus sit amet libero. Cras nisl neque, lacinia id, mollis vel, **dictum ac, ante.**

Read More

Dead Men's Money by J.S. Fletcher

Lorem ipsum dolor sit amet, consectetur adipiscing elit. Vestibulum commodo metus sit amet libero. Cras nisl neque, lacinia id, mollis vel, dictum ac, ante. Vestibulum tortor. **Lorem ipsum dolor sit amet.**

Read More

TOP BOOKS

Through the Looking Glass
by Lewis Carol

Princess of Mars
by Edgar Rice Burroughs

Through the Looking Glass
by Aesop

Gods of Mars
by Edgar Rice Burroughs

Chapters 7 through 11 use the example of a fictional site called voxLibris to show off various CSS techniques. I broke the code down and sometimes simplified it in those chapters.

This appendix includes the unexpurgated code—including all HTML and CSS—used to create the site. You can also download the code from:

speaking-in-styles.com/book

APPENDIX A

....

voxLibris Code

index.html

For details about
index.css, see Chapter
8, "Layout."

The content for the page is in the file *index.html*, which includes all of the HTML needed to create the structure of the page, but none of the styles. As with all HTML pages, it is composed of metadata between the *<head>* tags (03–07) and content between the *<body>* tags (08–139).

One other important note: I have included a break at the bottom of most rows and columns with the *alignclear* class, which stops floating:

<br class="alignclear"/>

For example, this code is included at line 15. This is needed in CSS to make sure that a parent element stretches to the full height of its children.

Books Should Be Free

The inspiration for voxLibris comes from a Web site called *booksshouldbefree.com*, which collects audio recordings of public domain books, making them available for free download.

```
01  <!DOCTYPE html PUBLIC "-//W3C//DTD
        XHTML 1.0 Strict//EN"z "http://www.
        w3.org/TR/xhtml1/DTD/xhtml1-strict.
        dtd">
02  <html xmlns="http://www.w3.org/1999/xhtml">
03  <head>
04  <meta http-equiv="Content-Type" content="text/
        html; charset=ISO-8859-1" />
05  <title>voxLIBRIS</title>
06  <link href="_css/main.css" rel="stylesheet"
        type="text/css" media="all"/>
07  </head>
08  <body>
09  <div id="page">
10  <div id="header" class="row">
11  <h1>voxLIBRIS</h1>
12  <div id="searchmain" class="section search">
13  <form>
14  <input type="text" value="search" />
15  <br class="alignclear" />
16  <select>
17  <option>titles</option>
18  <option>authors</option>
19  <option>full text</option>
20  </select>
21  </form>
22  </div>
23  </div>
24  <div id="content" class="row">
25  <div id="aside1" class="column">
26  <div id="menumain" class="section">
27  <h2>Welcome</h2>
28  <div class="content">
29  <p>voxLIBRIS provides public domain
        audiobooks you can download free of
        charge.</p>
30  <ul class="menu">
31  <li><a href="#">Genres</a></li>
32  <li><a href="#">About</a></li>
33  <li><a href="#">News</a></li>
34  <li><a href="#">Reviews</a></li>
35  <li><a href="#">Donate</a></li>
36  <li><a href="#">Contact</a></li>
37  </ul>
38  </div>
39  </div>
40  <div id="ads01" class="section ads">
41  <h2></h2>
42  <div class="content">
43  <p><strong>Top 50 WTF Comic Moments
        </strong><br />
44  Countdown The Most Outrageous Moments In
        Comic Book History!<br />
45  <a href="#">www.UGO.com/Comics</a></p>
46  <p><strong>HP Global Citizenship</
        strong><br />
47  Why Protecting Privacy is Essential For Socially
        Responsible Companies<br />
48  <a href="#">www.hp.com</a></p>
49  <p><strong>Environments</strong><br />
50  Find Environments & More Environments
        Options Here!<br />
51  <a href="#">Octopedia.com</a></p>
52  <p class="textalignright">Ads by <strong>Oogle
        </strong></p>
53  </div>
54  </div>
55  </div>
56  <div id="article1" class="column">
57  <div id="genrelist" class="section">
58  <h1>Genres</h1>
59  <ul class="genrelistbuttons">
60  <li class="genre-adventure">
        <a href="#"><em>Adventure </em>34
        books</a></li>
61  <li class="genre-anthropology">
        <a href="#"><em>Anthropology
        </em>12 books</a></li>
62  <li class="genre-children">
        <a href="#"><em>Children </em>90
        books</a></li>
63  <li class="genre-epic"><a href="#"><em>Epic
        </em>6 books</a></li>
64  <li class="genre-fantasy"><a
        href="#"><em>Fantasy </em>13 books
        </a></li>
65  <li class="genre-history"><a
        href="#"><em>History </em>46 books
        </a></li>
66  <li class="genre-humor"><a
        href="#"><em>Humor </em>18 books
        </a></li>
67  <li class="genre-medical">
        <a href="#"><em>Medical </em>21
        books
        </a></li>
68  <li class="genre-mystery">
        <a href="#"><em>Mystery </em>67
        books</a></li>
69  <li class="genre-philosophy">
        <a href="#"><em>Philosophy </em>2
        books</a></li>
```

index.html CONTINUED

```
70  <li class="genre-romance">
        <a href="#"><em>Romance </em>103
        books</a></li>
71  <li class="genre-scifi"><a href="#"><em>SciFi
        </em>54 books</a></li>
72  </ul>
73  <br class="alignclear" />
74  </div>
75  <div id="about" class="section">
76  <h2>About</h2>
77  <p>Nulla sed felis. Sed et tellus...</p>
78  <p>Suspendisse aliquam suscipit elit....
79  </p>
80  <p><a href="#" class="readmore">Read More
        </a></p>
81  </div>
82  <div id="news" class="section">
83  <h2>News</h2>
84  <div class="column">
85  <h3>voxLIBRIS Adds 30 New Books</h3>
86  <p>Lorem ipsum dolor sit amet...</p>
87  <p><a href="#" class="readmore">Read More
        </a></p>
88  </div>
89  <div class="column">
90  <h3>New Categories Coming Next Month</h3>
91  <p>Lorem ipsum dolo...</a></p>
92  </div>
93  <br class="alignclear" />
94  </div>
95  <div id="news" class="section">
96  <h2>Reviews</h2>
97  <div class="column">
98  <h3>Bowolf by Unknown</h3>
99  <p>Lorem ipsum dolor si...</p>
100 <p><a href="#" class="readmore">Read More
        </a></p>
101 </div>
102 <div class="column">
103 <h3>Dead Men's Money by J.S. Fletcher</h3>
104 <p>Lorem ipsum...</p><p><a href="#"
        class="readmore">Read More</a></p>
105 </div>
106 <br class="alignclear" />
107 </div>
108 </div>
109 <div id="aside2" class="column">
110 <div id="" class="section topbooks">
111 <h2>Top Books</h2>
112 <ul>
113 <li class="book alignleft"><a href="#">
        <img src="_images/bookcovers/
        small/through-the-looking-
        glass.jpg" alt="through-the-
        looking-glass" width="125"
        height="186"/><cite>Through the
        Looking Glass</cite>by Lewis Carol
        </a></li>
114
115 <li class="book alignleft"><a href="#">
        <img src="_images/bookcovers/small/
        Princess-of-Mars.jpg" alt="through-
        the-looking-glass" width="125"
        height="186"/><cite>Princess of Mars
        </cite>by Edgar Rice Burroughs
        </a></li>
116
117 <li class="book alignleft"><a href="#">
        <img src="_images/bookcovers/small/
        aesop-for-children.jpg" alt="through-
        the-looking-glass" width="125"
        height="186"/><cite>Aesop
        </cite>by Aesop</a></li>
118
119 <li class="book alignleft"><a href="#"><img
        src="_images/bookcovers/small/gods-of-
        mars.jpg" alt="Gods of Mars" width="125"
        height="186"/><cite>Gods of Mars
        </cite>by Edgar Rice Burroughs</a>
        </li>
120 </ul>
121 <br class="alignclear" />
122 </div>
123 </div>
124 <br class="alignclear" />
125 <div id="footer" class="row">
126 <div class="copyright">&copy; voxLIBRIS</div>
127 <ul class="menu">
128 <li><a href="#">Genres</a></li>
129 <li><a href="#">About</a></li>
130 <li><a href="#">News</a></li>
131 <li><a href="#">Reviews</a></li>
132 <li><a href="#">Donate</a></li>
133 <li><a href="#">Contact</a></li>
134 </ul>
135 <br class="alignclear" />
136 </div>
137 </div>
138 </div>
139 </body>
140 </html>
```

main.css

All external CSS code for *voxLibris* is imported into *main.css*, which is in turn linked to by *index.html*. During prototyping, it is often easiest to keep your CSS in several distinct files, using *@import* to add them to the master style sheet. This makes finding code easier, and makes switching between possible design concepts faster. For example, if you have a few different chrome concepts, you can simply switch the *chrome.css* file.

For details about *main.css*, see Chapter 8, "Layout."

Once you go into final deployment, however, I recommend copying and pasting all the CSS code into this file. This will speed up your page download and avoid some problems that IE has with using *@import*.

```
01  /*------------------------------------------------------------
02      Imported Styles
03  ------------------------------------------------------------*/
04  @import url(default.css);
05  @import url(layout.css);
06  @import url(navigation.css);
07  @import url(chrome.css);
```

default.css

For details about
default.css, see
Chapter 8, "Layout."

Default styles for the site reset the browser defaults—giving us a level playing field for the different browsers—and set site specific general styles for the HTML.

```
01  /*----------------------------------------------
02        Reset Browser Inherited Styles
03  ---------------------------------------------- */
04
05  html, body, div, span, applet, object, iframe, h1, h2,
        h3, h4, h5, h6, p, blockquote, pre, a, abbr,
        acronym, address, big, cite, code, del, dfn, em,
        font, img, ins, kbd, q, s, samp, small, strike,
        strong, sub, sup, tt, var, dd, dl, dt, li, ol, ul,
        fieldset, form, label, legend, table, caption,
        tbody, tfoot, thead, tr, th, td
06  {
07        margin: 0;
08        padding: 0;
09        border: 0;
10        outline: 0;
11        background: none;
12        font-weight: inherit;
13        font-style: inherit;
14        font-family: inherit;
15        font-size: 100%;
16        text-align: left;
17        vertical-align: baseline;
18        list-style: none;        }
```

```
19  /*----------------------------------------------
20        Default Styles
21  ---------------------------------------------- */
22  body, input, select {
23        color: rgb(105,105,105);
24        font-family: "fontin sans", optima, candara,
                "trebuchet-MS", sans-serif;        }
25
26  h1, h2, h3, h4, h5, h6 {
27        color: rgb(128,128,128);
28        font-family: garamond, cochin, cambria, times,
                serif;
29        letter-spacing: 1px;
30        font-weight: normal;        }
31
32  h1      {   font-size: 2.5em;   }
33  h2      {   font-size: 2em;     }
34  h3      {   font-size: 1.25em;  }
35  h4, h5, h6 { font-size: 1em; }
36  p       {
37        text-align: left;
38        font-size: .75em;
39        margin: 5px 0;
40        line-height: 1.5; }
41  blockquote {
42        font-size: .75em;
43        margin: 10px 0;
44        padding: 10px 0;
45        border-top: 1px solid rgb(128,128,128);
46        border-bottom: 1px solid rgb(128,128,128);
47        line-height: 1; }
48  li      {
49        font-size: .75em;
50        margin: 2px 0;        }
```

layout.css

The layout styles establish the layout grid in the design, defining how rows, columns, and sections should be placed.

For details about *layout.css*, see Chapter 8, "Layout."

```
01   /*---------------------------------------
02        Grid
03   ---------------------------------------*/
04   #page {
05        position: relative;
06        display: block;
07        margin:0 auto;
08        width: 980px;
09        _width: 960px;        }
10   /*---------------------------------------
11        Grid - Rows
12   ---------------------------------------*/
13   .row {
14        position: relative;
15        display: block;
16        margin:0 auto;        }
17   #header {    height: 100px;        }
18   #content {   padding-top: 20px; }
19   #footer {    height: 20px;        }
20   /*---------------------------------------
21        Grid - Columns
22   ---------------------------------------*/
23   .column {
24        position: relative;
25        display: block;
26        float: left;    }
27   .alignclear       {    clear: both; }
28   #aside1 {
29        top: 60px;
30        left: -80px;
31        width: 314px;         }
32   #article1 {
33        left: -40px;
34        width: 470px;         }
35   #aside2 {    width: 190px;       }

36   /*---------------------------------------
37        Grid - Sections
38   ---------------------------------------*/
39   .section {
40        position: relative;
41        display: block;          }
42   #header .search {
43        position: absolute;
44        right: 10px;
45        top: 10px;     }
46   #footer .copyright {
47        margin: 0 20px;
48        float: left; }
49   #aside1 .section {
50        width: 100%;
51        padding-bottom: 60px;     }
52   #aside1 .section h2 {
53        width: 100%;
54        padding: 80px 0 8px 18%;      }
55   #aside1 .section div.content {    width: 100%;        }
56   #aside1 .section p, #aside1 .section ul {
57        width: 65%;
58        margin: 0 auto;
59        margin-bottom: 5px;      }
60   #article1 .section .column {      width: 210px;      }
61   #article1 .section .column+.column {    float: right; }
62   #article1 .section .column p {    min-height: 110px;}
```

navigation.css

For details about
navigation.css,
see Chapter 10,
"Navigation."

All link, menu, and button styles are set in *navigation.css*.
Remember to set the styles for all of the different link states
(*:link*, *:visited*, *:active*, and *:hover*).

```
01  /*----------------------------------------
02        Links
03  ----------------------------------------*/
04  a            {     text-decoration: none;       }
05  a:link   {      color: rgb(0,85,126);         }
06  a:visited   {        color: rgb(0,50,75);       }
07  a:hover   {        color: rgb(0,170,255);     }
08  a:active{      color: rgb(255,215,0);     }
09  /*----------------------------------------
10        Links - Paragraph
11  ----------------------------------------*/
12  p a:link, p a:visited {
13        background: transparent url(../_images/bg-p-
            a-link.png) repeat-x 0 -2px;      }
14  p a:hover    {      background-position: -20px -2px;
15  p a:active    {      background-image: none; }
16
17  p a.readmore {
18        position: relative;
19        background: transparent url(../_images/icon-
            pointer-sprite.png) no-repeat right 0;
20        padding: 0 40px 5px 0;
21        _background: none;         }
22  p a.readmore:link {
23        background-position: right 0;       }
24  p a.readmore:visited {
25        background-position: right -20px;       }
26  p a.readmore:hover {
27        background-position: right -40px;       }
28  p a.readmore:active {
29        background-position: right -60px;       }

30  /*----------------------------------------
31        Menus
32  ----------------------------------------*/
33  ul.menu li a {
34        font-family: garamond, cochin, cambria, times,
            serif;
35        text-transform: uppercase; }
36  /*----------------------------------------
37        Menus - Menu
38  ----------------------------------------*/
39  #menumain ul.menu li {
40        display: block;
41        padding: 5px 0;
42        border-top: 1px solid rgb(192,192,192);
43        width: 100%; }
44  /*----------------------------------------
45        Navigation - Footer
46  ----------------------------------------*/
47  #footer ul.menu li {
48        float: left;
49        padding: 3px 20px;
50        margin: 0;
51        background: none;
52        border-left: 1px solid rgb(128,128,128);       }
53  #footer ul.menu li a:link, #footer ul.menu li a:visited {
            color: rgb(105,105,105);        }
```

```
54   /*------------------------------------------------------------
55           Article 1 - Genre List
56   ------------------------------------------------------------*/
57   #genrelist .genrelistbuttons { list-style: none; }
58   #genrelist .genrelistbuttons li {
59           background: none;
60           height: auto;
61           padding: 0;
62           font-size: .875em;
63           float: left;
64           text-align: center;
65           background: rgb(105,105,105) url(../_images/
                   genreicons/icon-adventure.jpg) no-repeat
                   center center;
66           display: block;
67           width: 100px;
68           height: 100px;
69           margin: 15px 15px 50px 0;
70           -webkit-border-radius: 10px;
71           -moz-border-radius: 10px;
72           border-radius: 10px;
73           -webkit-box-shadow: rgb(0,0,0) 0 0 5px;
74           -moz-box-shadow: rgb(0,0,0) 0 0 5px;
75           box-shadow: rgb(0,0,0) 0 0 5px;        }
76   #genrelist .genrelistbuttons li a {
77           display: block;
78           opacity: 1;
79           width: 100%;        background: transparent
                   url(../_images/button-gel-100.png) no-repeat
                   0 0;
80           padding-top: 105px;
81           color: rgb(169,169,169);
82           -webkit-border-radius: 10px;
83           -moz-border-radius: 10px;
84           border-radius: 10px;        }
85   #genrelist .genrelistbuttons li a em {
86           display: block;
87           margin-bottom: 5px;
88           font-style: normal;
89           line-height: 1;
90           font-size: 1.25em;
91           color: rgb(105,105,105);
92           font-family: garamond, cochin, cambria, times,
                   serif; }
93   #genrelist .genrelistbuttons li a:hover {
94           opacity: .6;
95           border-color: rgb(0,170,255);
96           color: rgb(0,0,0);     }
97   #genrelist .genrelistbuttons li.genre-adventure {
98           background-image: url(../_images/genreicons/
                   icon-adventure.jpg);     }
99   #genrelist .genrelistbuttons li.genre-anthropology {
100          background-image: url(../_images/genreicons/
                   icon-anthropology.jpg);  }
101  #genrelist .genrelistbuttons li.genre-children {
102          background-image: url(../_images/genreicons/
                   icon-children.jpg);       }
103  #genrelist .genrelistbuttons li.genre-epic {
104          background-image: url(../_images/genreicons/
                   icon-epic.jpg);     }
105  #genrelist .genrelistbuttons li.genre-fantasy {
106          background-image: url(../_images/genreicons/
                   icon-fantasy.jpg);  }
107  #genrelist .genrelistbuttons li.genre-history {
108          background-image: url(../_images/genreicons/
                   icon-history.jpg);  }
109  #genrelist .genrelistbuttons li.genre-humor {
110          background-image: url(../_images/genreicons/
                   icon-humor.jpg);  }
111  #genrelist .genrelistbuttons li.genre-medical {
112          background-image: url(../_images/genreicons/
                   icon-medical.jpg); }
113  #genrelist .genrelistbuttons li.genre-mystery {
114          background-image: url(../_images/genreicons/
                   icon-mystery.jpg); }
115  #genrelist .genrelistbuttons li.genre-philosophy {
116          background-image: url(../_images/genreicons/
                   icon-philosophy.jpg);     }
117  #genrelist .genrelistbuttons li.genre-romance {
118          background-image: url(../_images/genreicons/
                   icon-romance.jpg);      }
119  #genrelist .genrelistbuttons li.genre-scifi {
120          background-image: url(../_images/genreicons/
                   icon-scifi.jpg);     }
```

chrome.css

For details about
chrome.css, see
Chapter 11, "Chrome."

The site's visual appearance is set primarily by the *chrome.css* file.

```
01  /*-----------------------------------------
02          Chrome - Grid
03  -----------------------------------------*/
04  body { background: rgb(0,50,75) url(../_images/
          bg-body.png) repeat 0 0; }
05  #page {
06          background: transparent url(../_images/
              bg-page.png) repeat-y 0 0;
07          padding: 0 16px;
08
09          _background: none;
10          _filter: progid:DXImageTransform.Microsoft.
              AlphaImageLoader(src="../_images/bg-page.
              png", sizingMethod="scale"); }
11  #header, #footer {   background: transparent url(../_
          images/bg-header.png) repeat-x 0 0;   }
12  #footer {      background-position: 0 bottom;   }
13  /*-----------------------------------------
14          Chrome - Header - voxLIBRIS logo
15  -----------------------------------------*/
16  #header h1 {
17          position: absolute;
18          left: 0;
19          bottom: -2px;
20          width: 306px;
21          height: 66px;
22          line-height: 188px;
23          overflow: hidden;
24          background: transparent url(../_images/logo-
              voxlibris.png) no-repeat 0 0;
25          _background: none;
26          _filter: progid:DXImageTransform.Microsoft.
              AlphaImageLoader(src="../_images/logo-
              voxlibris.png', sizingMethod="crop');}

27  /*-----------------------------------------
28          Chrome - Header - Search
29  -----------------------------------------*/
30  #header .search input, #header .search select {
31          background: transparent url(../_images/
              bg-grad01.png) repeat-x center center;
32          border: 1px solid rgb(102,102,102);
33          height: 25px;
34          width: 200px;
35          font-size: 1.2em;
36          padding: 0 10px;
37          margin-bottom: 5px;
38          -moz-border-radius: 5px;
39          -webkit-border-radius: 5px;
40          border-radius: 5px; }
41  #header .search select {
42          background-image: url(../_images/bg-grad01.
              png);
43          padding-right: 0;   }
```

```
44   /*-----------------------------------------------------------
45          Chrome - Aside 1 - Section
46   -----------------------------------------------------------*/
47   #aside1 .section {
48       background: transparent url(../_images/
             bg-sidebar1-bottom.png) no-repeat 0 bottom;
             }
49   #aside1 .section h2 {
50       background: transparent url(../_images/
             bg-sidebar1-top.png) no-repeat 0 0;
51       text-align: left;
52       max-height: 136px;
53       overflow: hidden;
54       font-variant: small-caps;
55       color: red;    }
56   #aside1 .section div.content {
57       background: transparent url(../_images/
             bg-sidebar1-mid.png) repeat-y 0 0;     }
58   #aside1 .section p, #aside1 .section ul {
59       list-style-position: inside;
60       list-style-type: none;}
61   /*-----------------------------------------------------------
62          Chrome - Aside 1 - Ads
63   -----------------------------------------------------------*/
64   #aside1 .ads {
65       background-image: url(../_images/bg-ads-
             bottom.png);      }
66   #aside1 .ads h2 {
67       background-image: url(../_images/bg-ads-top.
             png);      }
68   #aside1 .ads div.content {
69       background-image: url(../_images/bg-ads-mid.
             png);      }
70   #aside1 .ads p {
71       color: rgb(0,0,0);
72       padding: 10px 80px;      }
```

```
73   /*-----------------------------------------------------------
74          Chrome - Article
75   -----------------------------------------------------------*/
76   #article1 .section h1 {
77       padding-top: 30px;
78       text-transform: uppercase;
79       text-align: center;
80       background: transparent url(../_images/
             flourish-up.png) no-repeat center top;  }
81   #article1 .section {
82       background-position: bottom center;
83       padding-bottom: 50px;
84       margin-bottom: 3px;
85       background: transparent url(../_images/
             flourish-up.png) no-repeat center bottom;    }
86   #article1 .section h2 {
87       font-variant: small-caps;
88       margin: 3px 0 30px 0;
89       height: 35px;
90       background: transparent url(../_images/
             flourish-down.png) no-repeat center 3px;
91       border-top: 1px solid rgb(128,128,128);      }
92   #article1 .section h3 {
93       font-family: "fontin sans", optima, candara,
             "trebuchet-MS", sans-serif;
94       height: 50px;
95       margin-top: 20px;  }
96   #article1 .section p {
97       margin-bottom: 20px;      }
98   #article1 ul li {
99       list-style: none;
100      list-style-position: inside;
101      background: transparent url(../_images/
             flourish-left.png) no-repeat 0 center;
102      padding: 10px 25px;
103      _background: none;
104      _filter: progid:DXImageTransform.Microsoft.
             AlphaImageLoader
105      (src="../_images/flourish-left.png",
             sizingMethod="crop|scale"); }
```

Web Safe Fonts

BETA-2

Font Name	Weight and Style	OS	Rank	Sample
Academy Engraved LET			3-Likely	ABCDEFGHIJKLMNOPQRSTUVWXYZ abcdefghijklmnopqrstuvwxyz 0123456789
Agency FB	bold		4-Less Likely	ABCDEFGHIJKLMNOPQRSTUVWXYZ abcdefghijklmnopqrstuvwxyz 0123456789
Algerian			4-Less Likely	ABCDEFGHIJKLMNOPQRSTUVWXYZ ABCDEFGHIJKLMNOPQRSTUVWXYZ 0123456789
American Typewriter	bold		2-Almost Certain	ABCDEFGHIJKLMNOPQRSTUVWXYZ abcdefghijklmnopqrstuvwxyz 0123456789
Andale Mono	bold, italic, bold/italic		1-Certain	ABCDEFGHIJKLMNOPQRSTUVWXYZ abcdefghijklmnopqrstuvwxyz 0123456789
Apple Chancery			2-Almost Certain	ABCDEFGHIJKLMNOPQRSTUVWXYZ abcdefghijklmnopqrstuvwxyz 0123456789
Apple Symbols			2-Almost Certain	ABCDEFGHIJKLMNOPQRSTUVWXYZ abcdefghijklmnopqrstuvwxyz 0123456789
Arial	bold, italic, bold/italic		1-Certain	ABCDEFGHIJKLMNOPQRSTUVWXYZ abcdefghijklmnopqrstuvwxyz 0123456789
Arial Black			1-Certain	ABCDEFGHIJKLMNOPQRSTUVWXYZ abcdefghijklmnopqrstuvwxyz 0123456789
Arial Narrow	bold, italic, bold/italic		3-Likely	ABCDEFGHIJKLMNOPQRSTUVWXYZ abcdefghijklmnopqrstuvwxyz 0123456789
Arial Rounded MT Bold	bold		3-Likely	ABCDEFGHIJKLMNOPQRSTUVWXYZ abcdefghijklmnopqrstuvwxyz 0123456789
Arial Unicode MS			4-Less Likely	ABCDEFGHIJKLMNOPQRSTUVWXYZ abcdefghijklmnopqrstuvwxyz 0123456789
Bank Gothic			3-Likely	ABCDEFGHIJKLMNOPQRSTUVWXYZ ABCDEFGHIJKLMNOPQRSTUVWXYZ 0123456789
Baskerville	bold, italic, bold/italic		2-Almost Certain	ABCDEFGHIJKLMNOPQRSTUVWXYZ abcdefghijklmnopqrstuvwxyz 0123456789
Baskerville Old Face			4-Less Likely	ABCDEFGHIJKLMNOPQRSTUVWXYZ abcdefghijklmnopqrstuvwxyz 0123456789
Bauhaus 93			4-Less Likely	ABCDEFGHIJKLMNOPQRSTUVWXYZ abcdefghijklmnopqrstuvwxyz 0123456789
Bell MT	bold, italic		4-Less Likely	ABCDEFGHIJKLMNOPQRSTUVWXYZ abcdefghijklmnopqrstuvwxyz 0123456789
Berlin Sans FB	bold		4-Less Likely	ABCDEFGHIJKLMNOPQRSTUVWXYZ abcdefghijklmnopqrstuvwxyz 0123456789
Berlin Sans FB Demi Bold			4-Less Likely	ABCDEFGHIJKLMNOPQRSTUVWXYZ abcdefghijklmnopqrstuvwxyz 0123456789
Bernard MT Condensed			4-Less Likely	ABCDEFGHIJKLMNOPQRSTUVWXYZ abcdefghijklmnopqrstuvwxyz 0123456789

In Chapter 6, we briefly discussed the values that could be used with different CSS properties. In this appendix, we'll look at values for lengths, fonts, URLs, and colors in more detail.

CSS VALUES

Lengths

Lengths (width or height) can be set using a variety of units, but there are two basic types of length values:

- **Relative lengths**: Length is calculated by the browser relative to another specific value.

- **Absolute lengths**: Lengths remain constant regardless of context but may vary depending on the computer's OS. For example, Macs have a slightly smaller value for point sizes than Windows.

Pixels or Ems?

Although you have several unit types to choose from, most Web designs are created using pixels or ems (or a combination of the two). Pixels have the advantage of being easy to understand and apply to screen-based layouts, but ems, a relative rather than absolute measurement, allow for more fluid control that can be gracefully scaled on most browsers.

Generally, I use pixels for all non-typographic lengths and ems for all font and text-based lengths.

Web-Safe Fonts

speaking-in-styles.com/web-typography/web-safe-fonts/

I have put together an extensive list of fonts that are likely to be installed on Mac and Windows machines. You can sort the list to see fonts with different weights and styles, OS, rank, as well as a sample of alpha-numeric characters.

Relative Length Values

Unit	Name	What It Is	Example
em	Em	Relative to the current font-size.	2.5em
ex	x-height	Relative to the distance between the baseline and the mean line of the font.	6ex
%	Percent	Relative to the length of parent element	19%
px	Pixel	Relative to the monitor's resolution.	603px

Absolute Length Values

Unit	Name	What It Is	Example
pt	Point	72pt = 1in	10pt
pc	Picas	1pc = 12pt	6pc
mm	Millimeters	1mm = .24pc	26mm
cm	Centimeters	1cm = 10mm	8.34cm
in	Inches	1in = 2.54cm	1.23in

Fonts

Font family names are derived from the name of the font. Entering the entire name as it appears in your operating system. Font names are not case-sensitive (it doesn't matter whether you use upper or lowercase letters), but font names with spaces must be placed in quotes:

"times new roman"

The table on the next few pages shows a list of fonts that are likely to be installed on both Macs and Windows computers.

For a complete list of Web-safe fonts that are likely to be installed on Mac or Windows computers, visit:

speaking-in-styles.com/web-typography/web-safe-fonts

Web-safe Fonts For Both Mac and Windows

Name	Weight & Style	Sample
Andale Mono	**Bold**, *Italic*, ***Bold Italic***	ABC abc 0123
Arial	**Bold**, *Italic*, ***Bold Italic***	ABC abc 0123
Arial Black		**ABC abc 0123**
Arial Narrow	**Bold**, *Italic*, ***Bold Italic***	ABC abc 0123
Arial Rounded MT Bold		**ABC abc 0123**
Baskerville Old Face		ABC abc 0123
Bauhaus 93		**ABC abc 0123**
Bell MT	**Bold**, *Italic*	ABC abc 0123
Bernard MT Condensed		**ABC abc 0123**
Book Antiqua	**Bold**, *Italic*, ***Bold Italic***	ABC abc 0123
Bookman Old Style	**Bold**, *Italic*, ***Bold Italic***	ABC abc 0123
Bradley Hand ITC TT	**Bold**	*ABC abc 0123*

Name	Weight & Style	Sample
Britannic Bold		ABC abc 0123
Brush Script MT		ABC abc 0123
Calibri	Bold, *Italic*, ***Bold Italic***	ABC abc 0123
Calisto MT	Bold, *Italic*, ***Bold Italic***	ABC abc 0123
Cambria	Bold, *Italic*, ***Bold Italic***	ABC abc 0123
Candara	Bold, *Italic*, ***Bold Italic***	ABC abc 0123
Century		ABC abc 0123
Century Gothic	Bold, *Italic*, ***Bold Italic***	ABC abc 0123
Century Schoolbook	Bold, *Italic*, ***Bold Italic***	ABC abc 0123
Colonna MT		ABC abc 0123
Comic Sans MS	Bold	ABC abc 0123
Consolas	Bold, *Italic*, ***Bold Italic***	ABC abc 0123
Constantia	Bold, *Italic*, ***Bold Italic***	ABC abc 0123
Cooper Black		ABC abc 0123
Copperplate Gothic Bold		ABC ABC 0123
Copperplate Gothic Light		ABC ABC 0123
Corbel	Bold, *Italic*, ***Bold Italic***	ABC abc 0123
Courier New		ABC abc 0123
Curlz MT		ABC abc 0123
Edwardian Script ITC		ABC abc 0123
Engravers MT		ABC ABC 0123
Footlight MT Light		ABC abc 0123
Franklin Gothic Book	*Italic*	ABC abc 0123
Franklin Gothic Medium	*Italic*	ABC abc 0123
Garamond	Bold, *Italic*	ABC abc 0123
Georgia	Bold, *Italic*, ***Bold Italic***	ABC abc 0123
Gill Sans MT	Bold, *Italic*, ***Bold Italic***	ABC abc 0123
Gill Sans Ultra Bold		ABC abc 0123
Gloucester MT Extra Condensed		ABC abc 0123

Name	Weight & Style	Sample
Goudy Old Style	**Bold**, *Italic*	ABC abc 0123
Haettenschweiler		ABC abc 0123
Harrington		ABC abc 0123
Impact		ABC abc 0123
Imprint MT Shadow		ABC abc 0123
Lucida Bright	**Bold**, *Italic*, ***Bold Italic***	ABC abc 0123
Lucida Calligraphy	**Bold**, *Italic*, ***Bold Italic***	ABC abc 0123
Lucida Console		ABC abc 0123
Lucida Fax	**Bold**, *Italic*, ***Bold Italic***	ABC abc 0123
Lucida Sans	**Bold**, *Italic*, ***Bold Italic***	ABC abc 0123
Lucida Sans Typewriter	**Bold**, *Italic*, ***Bold Italic***	ABC abc 0123
Lucida Sans Unicode		ABC abc 0123
Mistral		ABC abc 0123
MS Mincho		ABC abc 0123
MS Reference Sans Serif		ABC abc 0123
Onyx		ABC abc 0123
Papyrus		ABC abc 0123
Perpetua	**Bold**, *Italic*, ***Bold Italic***	ABC abc 0123
Perpetua Titling MT	**Bold**	ABC ABC 0123
Playbill		ABC abc 0123
Rockwell	**Bold**, *Italic*, ***Bold Italic***	ABC abc 0123
Rockwell Extra Bold		**ABC abc 0123**
Stencil		ABC ABC 0123
Tahoma	**Bold**	ABC abc 0123
Times New Roman	**Bold**, *Italic*, ***Bold Italic***	ABC abc 0123
Trebuchet MS	**Bold**, *Italic*, ***Bold Italic***	ABC abc 0123
Tw Cen MT	**Bold**, *Italic*, ***Bold Italic***	ABC abc 0123
Verdana	**Bold**, *Italic*, ***Bold Italic***	ABC abc 0123
Wide Latin		**ABC abc 0123**

URLs

A Uniform Resource Locator (URL) is the unique address of an item on the Web. It could be an HTML document, external CSS file, image, JavaScript file, Flash file, a sound file, or any resource that can be accessed by the Web browser. There are two types of URLs:

- **Absolute**: Gives the full address (path) of the resource, starting with *http://*. For example: *http://www.speaking-in-styles.com/story/images/rabbit.png* displays the file called *rabbit.png*.

- **Relative**: A partial path to the resource, relative to the file that is trying to use it. For example: *../images/rabbit.png* says to go up one directory level (*../*) into the images folder and load the file called *rabbit.png*.

Color

Colors in CSS are specified either by values specifying the mixture of red, green, and blue used to create the color, or with a specific color keyword. Keywords are simply shorthand for specific color values.

Color Opacity

Opacity is set as a property or can be included as part of the RGB Alpha color format, which includes a decimal value between 0 (transparent) and 1 (opaque). However, this is not currently supported by all browser. Include both the RGB and RGBA to cover all browsers:

color: rgb(255,0,0);
color: rgba(255,0,0,.5);

Format	Name	What It Is	Example
#RRGGBB	Hex	Red, green, and blue hexadecimal value of a color (00-99,AA-FF)	#CC33FF or #C3F
rgb(R#,G#,B#)	RGB Numeric	Red, green and blue numeric values of color (0-255)	rgb(204,51,255)
rgb(R%,G%,B%)	RGB Percentage	Red, green, and blue percentages	rgb(81%,18%,100%)
rgba(R,G,B,A)[1]	RGB Alpha	Red, green, and blue numeric values of color (numeric or percentage) and alpha value (0-1)	rgb(204,51,255,.5)
<name>	Keyword	A keyword name for the color	purple

[1] FF3+, GC1+, and Sa4+ only

Keyword	Hex	RGB Numeric	
aliceblue	#F0F8FF	240,248,255	
antiquewhite	#FAEBD7	250,235,215	
aqua	#00FFFF	0,255,255	
aquamarine	#7FFFD4	127,255,212	
azure	#F0FFFF	240,255,255	
beige	#F5F5DC	245,245,220	
bisque	#FFE4C4	255,228,196	
black	#000000	0,0,0	
blanchedalmond	#FFEBCD	255,235,205	
blue	#0000FF	0,0,255	
blueviolet	#8A2BE2	138,43,226	
brown	#A52A2A	165,42,42	
burlywood	#DEB887	222,184,135	
cadetblue	#5F9EA0	95,158,160	
chartreuse	#7FFF00	127,255,0	
chocolate	#D2691E	210,105,30	
coral	#FF7F50	255,127,80	
cornflowerblue	#6495ED	100,149,237	
cornsilk	#FFF8DC	255,248,220	
crimson	#DC143C	220,20,60	
cyan	#00FFFF	0,255,255	
darkblue	#00008B	0,0,139	
darkcyan	#008B8B	0,139,139	
darkgoldenrod	#B8860B	184,134,11	
darkgray	#A9A9A9	169,169,169	
darkgreen	#006400	0,100,0	
darkgrey	#A9A9A9	169,169,169	
darkkhaki	#BDB76B	189,183,107	
darkmagenta	#8B008B	139,0,139	
darkolivegreen	#556B2F	85,107,47	
darkorange	#FF8C00	255,140,0	

Color *continued*

Keyword	Hex	RGB Numeric	
darkorchid	#9932CC	153,50,204	
darkred	#8B0000	139,0,0	
darksalmon	#E9967A	233,150,122	
darkseagreen	#8FBC8F	143,188,143	
darkslateblue	#483D8B	72,61,139	
darkslategray	#2F4F4F	47,79,79	
darkturquoise	#00CED1	0,206,209	
darkviolet	#9400D3	148,0,211	
deeppink	#FF1493	255,20,147	
deepskyblue	#00BFFF	0,191,255	
dimgray	#696969	105,105,105	
dimgrey	#696969	105,105,105	
dodgerblue	#1E90FF	30,144,255	
firebrick	#B22222	178,34,34	
floralwhite	#FFFAF0	255,250,240	
forestgreen	#228B22	34,139,34	
fuchsia	#FF00FF	255,0,255	
gainsboro	#DCDCDC	220,220,220	
ghostwhite	#F8F8FF	248,248,255	
gold	#FFD700	255,215,0	
goldenrod	#DAA520	218,165,32	
gray	#808080	128,128,128	
green	#008000	0,128,0	
greenyellow	#ADFF2F	173,255,47	
grey	#808080	128,128,128	
honeydew	#F0FFF0	240,255,240	
hotpink	#FF69B4	255,105,180	
indianred	#CD5C5C	205,92,92	
indigo	#4B0082	75,0,130	
ivory	#FFFFF0	255,255,240	
khaki	#F0E68C	240,230,140	

Keyword	Hex	RGB Numeric	
lavender	#E6E6FA	230,230,250	
lavenderblush	#FFF0F5	255,240,245	
lawngreen	#7CFC00	124,252,0	
lemonchiffon	#FFFACD	255,250,205	
lightblue	#ADD8E6	173,216,230	
lightcoral	#F08080	240,128,128	
lightcyan	#E0FFFF	224,255,255	
lightgoldenrodyellow	#FAFAD2	250,250,210	
lightgray	#D3D3D3	211,211,211	
lightgreen	#90EE90	144,238,144	
lightgrey	#D3D3D3	211,211,211	
lightpink	#FFB6C1	255,182,193	
lightsalmon	#FFA07A	255,160,122	
lightseagreen	#20B2AA	32,178,170	
lightskyblue	#87CEFA	135,206,250	
lightslategray	#778899	119,136,153	
lightslategrey	#778899	119,136,153	
lightsteelblue	#B0C4DE	176,196,222	
lightyellow	#FFFFE0	255,255,224	
lime	#00FF00	0,255,0	
limegreen	#32CD32	50,205,50	
linen	#FAF0E6	250,240,230	
magenta	#FF00FF	255,0,255	
maroon	#800000	128,0,0	
mediumaquamarine	#66CDAA	102,205,170	
mediumblue	#0000CD	0,0,205	
mediumorchid	#BA55D3	186,85,211	
mediumpurple	#9370DB	147,112,219	
mediumseagreen	#3CB371	60,179,113	
mediumslateblue	#7B68EE	123,104,238	
mediumspringgreen	#00FA9A	0,250,154	

Color *continued*

Keyword	Hex	RGB Numeric	
mediumturquoise	#48D1CC	72,209,204	
mediumvioletred	#C71585	199,21,133	
midnightblue	#191970	25,25,112	
mintcream	#F5FFFA	245,255,250	
mistyrose	#FFE4E1	255,228,225	
moccasin	#FFE4B5	255,228,181	
navajowhite	#FFDEAD	255,222,173	
navy	#000080	0,0,128	
oldlace	#FDF5E6	253,245,230	
olive	#808000	128,128,0	
olivedrab	#6B8E23	107,142,35	
orange	#FFA500	255,165,0	
orangered	#FF4500	255,69,0	
orchid	#DA70D6	218,112,214	
palegoldenrod	#EEE8AA	238,232,170	
palegreen	#98FB98	152,251,152	
paleturquoise	#AFEEEE	175,238,238	
palevioletred	#DB7093	219,112,147	
papayawhip	#FFEFD5	255,239,213	
peachpuff	#FFDAB9	255,218,185	
peru	#CD853F	205,133,63	
pink	#FFC0CB	255,192,203	
plum	#DDA0DD	221,160,221	
powderblue	#B0E0E6	176,224,230	
purple	#800080	128,0,128	
red	#FF0000	255,0,0	
rosybrown	#BC8F8F	188,143,143	
royalblue	#4169E1	65,105,225	
saddlebrown	#8B4513	139,69,19	
salmon	#FA8072	250,128,114	
sandybrown	#F4A460	244,164,96	

Keyword	Hex	RGB Numeric	
seagreen	#2E8B57	46,139,87	
seashell	#FFF5EE	255,245,238	
sienna	#A0522D	160,82,45	
silver	#C0C0C0	192,192,192	
skyblue	#87CEEB	135,206,235	
slateblue	#6A5ACD	106,90,205	
slategray	#708090	112,128,144	
slategrey	#708090	112,128,144	
snow	#FFFAFA	255,250,250	
springgreen	#00FF7F	0,255,127	
steelblue	#4682B4	70,130,180	
tan	#D2B48C	210,180,140	
teal	#008080	0,128,128	
thistle	#D8BFD8	216,191,216	
tomato	#FF6347	255,99,71	
turquoise	#40E0D0	64,224,208	
violet	#EE82EE	238,130,238	
wheat	#F5DEB3	245,222,179	
white	#FFFFFF	255,255,255	
whitesmoke	#F5F5F5	245,245,245	
yellow	#FFFF00	255,255,0	
yellowgreen	#9ACD32	154,205,50	

Compatibility
QuirksBlog
About

Page last changed 6 weeks ago

þp]{ sitemap contact

Search QuirksMode.or Search

show site navigation

CSS contents and browser compatibility

show page contents

The contents of my CSS pages and browser compatibility.

Table of Contents

Last major update on 28 March 2009.

Mobile table.

See the CSS Selector Test for tests of and information about CSS3 selectors.

Quirks and Strict mode	How to trigger them, what the differences are. Contains compatibility table.
CSS Hacks	Be very, very careful.
Conditional comments	A generally reliable method for separating IE from all other browsers.

Earlier versions of this page has been translated into Brazilian Portuguese and Romanian.

CSS 2.1 selectors

Specification.

Contents of this table ⇕ See also the key to my compatibility tables.

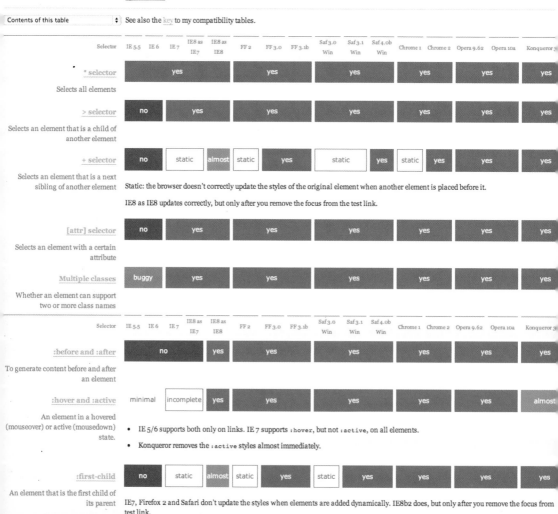

Selector	IE 5.5	IE 6	IE 7	IE8 as IE7	IE8 as IE8	FF 2	FF 3.0	FF 3.1b	Saf 3.0 Win	Saf 3.1 Win	Saf 4.0b Win	Chrome 1	Chrome 2	Opera 9.62	Opera 10a	Konqueror 3
* selector Selects all elements	yes	yes	yes	yes	yes	yes	yes	yes	yes	yes	yes	yes	yes	yes	yes	yes
> selector Selects an element that is a child of another element	no	yes	yes	yes	yes	yes	yes	yes	yes	yes	yes	yes	yes	yes	yes	yes
+ selector Selects an element that is a next sibling of another element	no	static	static	almost	static	yes	yes	static	yes	yes	static	yes	yes	yes	yes	yes

Static: the browser doesn't correctly update the styles of the original element when another element is placed before it.

IE8 as IE8 updates correctly, but only after you remove the focus from the test link.

Selector																
[attr] selector Selects an element with a certain attribute	no	yes	yes	yes	yes	yes	yes	yes	yes	yes	yes	yes	yes	yes	yes	yes
Multiple classes Whether an element can support two or more class names	buggy	yes	yes	yes	yes	yes	yes	yes	yes	yes	yes	yes	yes	yes	yes	yes

Selector	IE 5.5	IE 6	IE 7	IE8 as IE7	IE8 as IE8	FF 2	FF 3.0	FF 3.1b	Saf 3.0 Win	Saf 3.1 Win	Saf 4.0b Win	Chrome 1	Chrome 2	Opera 9.62	Opera 10a	Konqueror 3
:before and :after To generate content before and after an element	no		yes	yes	yes	yes	yes	yes	yes	yes	yes	yes	yes	yes	yes	yes
:hover and :active An element in a hovered (mouseover) or active (mousedown) state.	minimal	incomplete	yes	yes	yes	yes	yes	yes	yes	yes	yes	yes	yes	yes	yes	almost

- IE 5/6 supports both only on links. IE 7 supports :hover, but not :active, on all elements.
- Konqueror removes the :active styles almost immediately.

Selector																
:first-child An element that is the first child of its parent	no	static	almost	static	yes	static	yes		yes			yes		yes		yes

IE7, Firefox 2 and Safari don't update the styles when elements are added dynamically. IE8b2 does, but only after you remove the focus from test link.

In Chapter 3, Myth 3 mentions that, although there are still some compatibility issues between the different browsers, the main culprit is Internet Explorer with version 6 being the most troublesome. Although newer versions (7 and 8) have improved on their predecessor, they have their issues as well.

Fixing the problems in IE used to consume a lot of my time. Knowing the problems are primarily created by CSS quirks in IE, I now rely on three basic fixes to get my designs to work across all browsers.

Appendix C

Fixing Internet Explorer

Understanding Quirks

As I have mentioned throughout this book, CSS is an inter-
preted language. The browser manufacturers take the standard
and implement it to the best of their abilities. However, older
browsers were often created before the standards had been fully
defined. When the browser maker implemented a standard differently from the way it was later specified by the W3C, it's called
a *quirk*.

IE5 had a lot of quirks compared with modern browsers.
Although IE5 is not commonly used anymore and IE6 fixed
many of these problems, in order to allow backwards compatibility, Microsoft implemented a *quirks mode* in IE6 where it emu-
lated IE5's CSS. Unfortunately, quirks mode is easily triggered
in IE6, causing a lot of design problems—most notably the box
model problem described in Chapter 6, "Vocabulary."

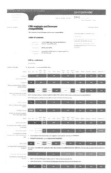

Quirks Mode

quirksmode.com

For a complete list of which CSS properties
and values work in which browsers, there is
no better resource than Peter-Paul Koch's
Quirks Mode site. Peter-Paul keeps it up to
date with the latest browsers, bugs, and
solutions.

Fix 1: Doctype Switching

The simplest solution to IE quirks is to declare a Doctype at the top of your HTML, defining the version of HTML or XHTML you are using. This is generally set by the developer when they create the HTML, but if you are doing your own development, I recommend sticking with XHTML transitional:

<!DOCTYPE html PUBLIC "-//W3C//DTD XHTML 1.0 Transitional//EN" "http://www.w3.org/TR/xhtml1/DTD/ xhtml1-transitional.dtd">

In theory, this will force IE6 to use modern CSS standards, so you will have to do very little tweaking to your code to get your designs to conform to multiple browsers.

Unfortunately, if your code does not conform to the version you specify (e.g., there are any syntax errors), IE6 will automatically kick into quirks mode. So, unless you know your code will be perfectly formed and without error, this is not a practical solution.

Fix 2: Conditional Styles

One advantage IE has over other browsers is that you can define styles that only IE can see, even tailored for a particular version. To add *conditional styles*, use this HTML code:

```
<!--[if IE 6]>
<link src="css/ie6.css" type="text/css" media="all" />
<![endif]-->
```

This will load the style sheet *ie6.css* only if the browser being used is IE6. You can replace the "6" in *if IE6* with another version number or leave it out entirely and the style sheet will affect all versions of IE.

You can now place any styles you want in the external file to "fix" any problems you see in the Web page. For example, you might include different padding to fix the box model problem described in Chapter 6.

The disadvantage of using conditional styles is that it means linking to more files (slowing down your Web page) and having to keep up with changes to more files.

Fix 3: Underscore Hack

Although possibly the least elegant solution, the underscore hack is the simplest and most direct IE fix. Place an underscore character immediately before a line of CSS code that you want only IE6 to see, and it is hidden from all other browsers. For example:

width: 250px;
padding: 25px;
_width: 300px;

If the browser is in quirks mode, this will reset the width of the box from 250px to 300px so it will appear to be the same width in IE6 as in other browsers.

The downsides to the underscore hack are that it only works in IE6 (not in newer versions), it will prevent your code from validating with the W3C CSS validator, and, if your browser is not in *quirks mode*, the values will be wrong, so its best to reserve this technique until after you try Fix.

Common IE6 Issues

Although on it's way out, IE6 still has to be reckoned with. I've spent a lot of time fixing IE6 compatibility problems, and want to share the most common with you, along with which fix to use.

See "Box" in Chapter 6, "Vocabulary," for more details on the box model, margins, and floating.

- **The Box Model**: The width or height of an element appears longer than in other browsers.
  FIX: If Doctype switching does not work, use conditional styles or the underscore hack to set a separate length.

- **Doubling Margins**: The margins on floated elements are doubled.
  FIX: If Doctype switching does not work, use conditional styles or the underscore hack to set separate margins.

- **Stair-Step Elements**: Instead of having their tops line up, floated elements look stair-stepped, with each subsequent floated element lower than the previous.
  FIX: Set the line height of the parent element to 0.

No Min/Max Width or Min/Max Height: Before version 7, IE did not support the *min-width*, *max-width*, *min-height*, or *max-height* properties.

FIX: Set conditional styles with the underscore hack to set absolute width or height. The good news is that IE6 treats *height* the way modern browsers treat *min-height*.

See "Width and Height" in Chapter 6, "Vocabulary," for more details on widths and heights.

No Support for Dynamic Pseudo-Classes: Although IE6 supports pseudo-classes with links (*<a>*), it does not support pseudo-class styles applied to any other HTML tags. This is generally not a problem (the extra styles can be treated as a design enhancement), but if you are using an opacity or lighter colors in the non-active state, expecting the dynamic action to darken the element when in use, this can cause problems.

FIX: Use conditional styles or the underscore hack to set an appropriate default color or opacity.

See "Styles for Special Cases" in Chapter 4, "Syntax," for more details on pseudo-classes.

No Alpha Support for PNG: Although it will display PNG images, IE6 fills any alpha channel with a muddy gray.

FIX: Use conditional styles or the underscore hack to set a non-transparent PNG source image, or, if the image is in the background, load the image using the IE alpha filter.

See "Using Transparent Images" in Chapter 11, "Chrome," for more details on transparent PNGs.

Index

and link pseudo-classes, 80
making changes based on, 180
and mood boards, 188
user interface, 192
UXBooth, 250

V

Validation Service, W3C CSS, 274, 276, 277, 321
validator.w3.org, 275
values
as component of style rules, 52
types of, 124–125
variables, 125
Verdana font, 226, 227
vertical-align property, 132, 133
vertical menus, 248, 251
video, 14
visibility, 144–145
visibility value, 144, 145
visited state, 80, 81, 82, 244, 298
visual comps
adjusting margins/padding in, 186
comparing with actual Web site, 26
cutting chrome from, 192
and fluid typography, 232
purpose of, 190
and site-planning process, 180
static *vs.* dynamic, 82
tips for creating, 190
voxLibris
code for, 291–301
inspiration for, 292
as model for design process, 180

W

W3C
and CSS, 44
CSS Validation Service, 274, 276, 277, 321
CSS Work Group, 158

jargon, 255
meaning of acronym, 44
Web applications, 30–33
Web browsers, 18–23. *See also* specific browsers
alternatives to leading, 22, 23
and CSS, 18, 20–21, 44, 317
and design enhancements, 172, 254
and downloadable fonts, 230
and font sizes, 236
graphics-based, 8
layout engines for, 23
legacy, 18
Macintosh, 18, 20–21
most commonly used, 18
and outlines, 174
and rounded corners, 174
and shadows, 172
viewing Web page on different, 19
Windows, 20–21
Web design, 179–207
adapting for print, 281
best practices, 284
and browser viewport, 150
building site, 192–203
choosing tools for, 17
deploying site, 204–205
vs. designing for other media, 150, 180
dynamic nature of, 180
as iterative process, 180, 206–207
making CSS central part of, 179
overview of process, 180–181
page-flow considerations, 184–185
planning phase, 182–191
source of news and updates on, 2
standards, 275
testing, 196
tools. *See* Web designer's toolbox
Web Designer Wall, 34, 36
Web designer's toolbox, 17–34
code editors, 28–29
design ideas, 34
Firefox add-ons, 24–27
online tools, 30–33
tutorials, 34

Safari
Books Online

Get free online access
to this book for 45 days!

And get access to thousands more by signing up for a free trial to Safari Books Online!

With the purchase of this book you have instant online, searchable access to it for 45 days on Safari Books Online! And while you're there, be sure to check out Safari Books Online's on-demand digital library and their free trial offer (a separate sign-up process). Safari Books Online subscribers have access to thousands of technical, creative and business books, instructional videos, and articles from the world's leading publishers.

Simply visit www.peachpit.com/safarienabled and enter code JNZJSAA to try it today.